PAINTING

THE

TOWN SILVER

PAINTING THE TOWN SILVER

The life and times of Leslie Silver OBE

John Fisher

BEECROFT PUBLICATIONS

2015

Painting the Town Silver

Copyright © John Fisher 2014

Published in 2015 by
Beecroft Publications
72 Waterloo Lane
Bramley, Leeds
LS13 2JF
www.beecroftpublications.co.uk

A CIP catalogue record for this book is available from the
British Library.

ISBN 978-0-9930909-0-5

Design and typography by Elizabeth Bee (c) 2014

Front cover design by Joe Bean at Print Ideas Ltd, Devonshire
House, Devonshire Ave, Leeds LS8 1AY

Printed and bound in the Great Britain by
CPI Group (UK) Ltd, Croydon, CR0 4YY

This book is dedicated to the
memory of Isaac Meyer Zylberstäjn,
whose decision to leave Poland enabled his family to
survive and this story to be told

Slowly, silently, now the moon
walks the night in her silver shoon;
This way, and that, she peers, and sees
Silver fruit upon silver trees

Walter de la Mare (1873-1956)

Contents

Illustrations

Acknowledgements

To Hilary for her research and supervision of the project, to Jane and Mark and family members for their input and to Peter Curwen for his invaluable help and advice.

With grateful thanks for their co-operation in providing anecdotes to Dr Jeffrey Sherwin and Professor Leslie Wagner and to many staff of the original Silver Paint and Lacquer Company Ltd.

Thanks also to David Bransby for his help with the photographs.

The photograph of the Leeds United Victory parade on page 93 is reproduced with the kind permission of Johnston Press.

Foreword

Leslie Silver was the epitome of all that was good about 'old style' football club ownership.

He was a hugely successful, self-made, entrepreneurial spirit who never lost sight of his solid East End, working class roots. Leslie rarely spoke about his past and only on very rare occasions might he be persuaded to recall, with great reluctance, his wartime experiences as a bomber navigator in the RAF.

Leslie was old school – a shy, sensitive, modest, considerate and loyal gentleman. However, behind all that gentleness there was a core of steely determination and courage. He was never afraid to make a big decision and when he did, he saw it through.

Later in his life, his hard-earned wealth allowed him to enjoy a more affluent lifestyle which took him far away from the sort of community in which he'd spent his childhood; yet in spirit he never disowned those roots and was always very much at home alongside those with whom he had once lived and worked.

In addition to building his paint business and his work at Leeds United, his contribution to a whole range of other diverse Leeds initiatives was immense.

For a football manager he was the ideal chairman – when you needed him he was there but never ever was he in your hair. He managed to remain one of Leeds United's biggest, most enthusiastic and, yes, at times childlike fans.

Nevertheless, at the same time he recognised that being chairman carried a huge responsibility which often precluded him from many of those privileges he used to enjoy so much when he was just a fan.

When I first met Leslie, Leeds United was in a sorry mess. They didn't own the ground or the inadequate training ground at Elland Road. They were in debt and fourth bottom of the Second Division, with six points from nine games. When I left Leeds, eight years later, we owned a magnificent stadium, had built and owned the world class academy training facility at Thorpe Arch and were very solid financially. Leslie, ably assisted by fellow directors Bill Fotherby, Peter Gilman and myself had managed to turn the club on its head.

In seven full seasons we had won two championships, finished fourth once and fifth twice in the top league, we'd won the Charity Shield, endured a losing appearance in the League Cup Final and qualifications for the European Cup.

I am convinced that were it not for the horrendous armed robbery he and Sheila were made to endure, the decision to sell the club would not have been taken. I am also equally convinced that if that had been the case, there is every chance we would have emulated the exploits of Manchester United.

I am sure most readers will pick up this book expecting to read about Leslie Silver, the football man. What pleases me enormously is the fact that this book tells us much more. John Fisher allows us to see beyond the football and enter the remarkable world of Leslie Silver, the person.

Leslie was a man of many talents, but most of all he was a people person and as such a man respected by all who knew him. To my wife Sam and I, Leslie and his delightful wife Sheila were always friends first, chairman and wife second.

This book is a belated fitting tribute to a great bloke who has given so much and asked for so little in return.

HOWARD WILKINSON
May 2014

Preface

Given the circumstances of Leslie Howard Silverstein's background in the East End of London in 1925, the year of his birth, no one could ever have predicted that a schoolboy who was advised to leave his place of education at the age of fourteen because he "wouldn't amount to much", would have gone on to become one of Leeds' leading benefactors.

His support and work for many worthwhile causes and institutions, notably in civic life, sport, education, art and theatre, have been exemplary. His foresight, tenacity and audacity allowed him to become a pioneer in the Yorkshire paint industry which eventually transformed him into an outstanding philanthropic industrialist.

I hope the tale that unfolds – a quintessential rags to riches story if ever there was one – will inform, amuse and inspire the reader. Here is a celebration of the life of a man, modest, affable and generous to a fault, whose epitaph could very well be headed, "I don't know what all the fuss was about."

JOHN FISHER

Leslie, aged 9 months

One

Family Matters

THE TWENTIES WAS THAT astonishingly quirky era often portrayed as the Roaring Twenties or the Jazz Age with its dazzling dreams and dubious morality. In the East End of London in the mid-1920s one could, and generally did, perceive the decade in a somewhat different light. The decade was characterized by the rise of political movements and the elevation of the far right and fascism, which was seen as the solution to prevent the spread of communism, but to the Jewish community in particular this state of affairs was viewed as a disturbing threat.

Severne Street was situated in the area just south of Commercial Street, a major arterial road in Tower Hamlets, in the east end of London, that runs from Shoreditch High Street to Whitechapel High Street. Today the area is highly built up and although it has become more fashionable it still maintains its busy commercial ambience.

Severne Street was an East End thoroughfare that was typical of the few square miles of overcrowded, grim and unsanitary back-to-back housing of that period. It comprised a long through road of drab, gardenless terrace houses. Open the front door of any dwelling and one stepped into a long narrow corridor which gave access to a parlour, a backroom and a kitchen which itself opened out onto a courtyard where there was an outside lavatory and a water supply from a pipe in the wall. Walk up the narrow stairway inside and usually you came to three small cramped bedrooms.

The typical dwelling had no electricity and lighting was provided by a gas lamp. It was cold and damp in the winter and unbearably hot and stuffy in the summer; a house ill equipped at any season for the impoverished family who lived there.

This was an area that often was referred to as 'darkest London' in Victorian times where nearby Whitechapel had been the hub of East End life. In the second half of the 19th century, Spitalfields had become the home for Dutch and German Jews and later a safe haven for the masses of disadvantaged Polish and Russian Jewish immigrants whose lives were in danger and who, taking a leap of faith, flocked to Britain's shores.

Leslie Howard Silverstein was born in Waterloo Road in the East End on 22 January 1925, some fifteen months after his parents Harry Silverstein and Bessie Hoffman were married. Right from being a baby, Leslie was a frequent visitor to Severne Street, Back Church Lane, where both sets of grandparents lived in adjacent houses. He was treated as the family's young bundle of love and a great fuss was made over him.

The Severne Street dwellings became the family hub where an open door welcomed everybody. These early days were to make a vivid impression on Leslie. The most significant influences on the first part of his life stemmed from the close-knit community; its affection, generosity and social values and specifically its love of family life. These were to pave the way for a heritage he celebrated throughout his life; this then was the legacy that would spur him on to achieve great things.

Today the East End of Leslie's childhood has mostly vanished. However, although many streets have not survived, including Severne Street, the vibrancy and intensity of communal life still remains. It was a friendly neighbourhood – the street filled with Jewish and Irish families who lived on opposite sides of the street to each other. Their lives were broadly compatible although there was some confusion, particularly at the weekends. This was mainly because the Irish drank a lot more liquor than the Jews. It was not a segregated area by any means and neighbours of all denominations lived together without conflict, which was remarkable considering the times.

Christian neighbours would often be employed as domestic cleaners and many, known as *Shabbos goys*, would be invited into Jewish homes on the Sabbath to light coal fires when it was forbidden by religious law for a Jew to do so. They welcomed some extra cash, albeit merely pennies, and the chance to help neighbours from another faith. The Jews were good neighbours and wanted to live in peace. But on Saturday and Sunday nights the place erupted into an inebriated, unruly area where the sound of shouting in the streets was mixed with raucous Irish laughter and occasional brawling and punch-ups which tended to abate into calm stillness in the early hours of the morning.

Irish eyes were continually smiling but in the case of the Jews, eyes were constantly watching for political eruptions and anti-Semitic outbursts as they had done ever since Jewish immigrants had landed in Britain in the middle of the 19th and the turn of the 20th centuries.

The Aliens Act of 1905 had introduced, for the first time, immigration controls and registration, giving the Home Secretary overall responsibility for immigration and nationality matters. One of its main objectives was to control Jewish immigration from eastern Europe where Jews were fleeing from racial persecution. The Act was designed to prevent 'paupers or criminals' from entering the country and set up a mechanism to deport those who slipped through the system.

In 1905, an editorial in the Manchester Evening Chronicle wrote that "the dirty, destitute, diseased, verminous and criminal foreigner who dumps himself on our soil and rates simultaneously shall be forbidden to land." Racial hatred was rife against and amongst the Jewish immigrants who settled in communities such as Leeds, Manchester and elsewhere. But it was no more intense than the racial hatred that existed in some parts of the East End of London. Public demonstrations, under the auspices of the British Brothers League in favour of restricting further immigration of destitute foreigners into Great Britain, were often held in the East End. One such protest was held at the People's Palace in Mile End in 1902 under the chairmanship of Major Evans-Gordon MB who was supported by members of parliament.

By the time Leslie was four years old the Roaring Twenties had shouted itself hoarse and began to make way for a newer voice – the Great Depression.

૱ ૱ ૱

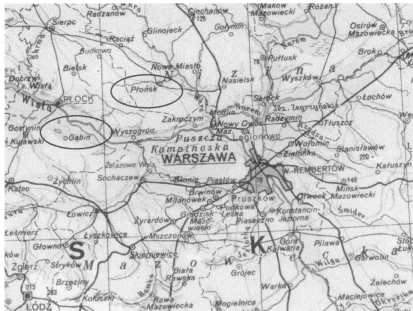

Map showing
Gombin (Gabin)
and Plonsk
north west of
Warsaw

Leslie's paternal *bobba* (grandmother) Sarah (Chaya Soorah), the daughter of Reb Oosher Ticerchinksy, and his paternal *zayda* (grandfather) Isaac (Yitzchok) Meyer, the son of Sholoma Zalma Zylberstäjn (spelt with an umlaut above the 'a') had originally come from Gombin in Poland towards the end of the 19th century. Gombin, known as Gabin in Polish, was a small town about sixty kilometres north west of Warsaw, which had a thriving Jewish settlement dating from the 15th century. At the end of the 19th century, the Jewish population was engaged in all aspects of trade, commerce and tailoring as well as the fur trade, with numerous religious, educational and cultural organisations. In 1897 there were 2,539 Jews in the town of 5,137.

The large Silverstein family consisted of six sons – Asher (Ashy, who was born in Gombin), Harry (Leslie's father), Joe, Dave, Eli and Max (who died young) – and two daughters, Betty and Hannah.

There was also an adopted daughter whom Sarah and Isaac fostered when the rabbi of the nearest synagogue pleaded for a home for a destitute child from the East End. Isaac heard of the news at the morning synagogue service. The infant was a neighbour's newly-orphaned offspring, and if no-one would take her in she would be compelled to enter a non-Jewish orphanage. With typical generosity,

Paternal grandparents – Sarah and Isaac Meyer Silverstein

Maternal grandparents – Hannah and Shmuel Meir Hoffman

quiet concern and dignity, Isaac immediately offered to take the child to live with his family. He made the necessary arrangements and came back with the girl and calmly laid a place at the dining table where she could sit with the family.

She stayed in the household as a foster child but was always treated as one of the clan. She, in turn, always referred to Isaac and Sarah as her 'mamma and dadda'. Her name was Anne Burke and she lived with Silversteins until she married.

Sadly, it was not to prove an easy time for Anne after she left the security of her adopted home and family. Anne's first husband, who served in the army during the Second World War, was killed on active service and when Anne remarried things certainly didn't improve. Her second husband endured poor health which led to a serious, chronic illness and Anne tended to his every need until he died prematurely.

Isaac Meyer Silverstein
in Severne Street

Leslie's grandfather Isaac was a tailor, however, in the old country and when he first arrived in London he was a 'milk carrier' which is better known in more modern terms as a milkman. He was ultra-orthodox and a *baal kora* – a person who chants the weekly *sedra* (portion of Law) from the scrolls of law known as the *Sefer Torah*. He *davened* (prayed) in the preposterously named Christian Street Talmud Torah synagogue, just off Commercial Road. The street was, in actual fact, named after Fletcher Christian who led the mutiny on the Bounty.

Although the family was poor, Isaac refused to accept a fee as *baal kora* as he didn't believe one should be paid for performing a *mitzvah* (a good deed). One Passover, Isaac was employed as a *shomer* (a religious supervisor) who oversaw the cleansing and change-over of food and utensils for Passover in Jewish cafes and shops where food was served. For Isaac this went very much against the grain; he told his family later that he would never do the job again as he was expected to turn a blind eye to the less than stringent preparations being conducted before him. Nevertheless, for an orthodox Jew he was tolerant, especially towards his own family. On Sabbath afternoons he would pretend to be asleep in his chair so as not to confront his less observant children as they sneaked out of the house.

Harry Silverstein came into the world in London on 22 March 1899 while Bessie, born in Plonsk, came to England as a Polish immigrant and a child in arms. No Polish birth certificate can be found for Bessie but taking the place of the missing documentation there exists an English deed originating from the Thames Police Court and signed by her mother Hannah. She wrote: "I Hannah Hoffman, 23 Severne Street, Back Church Lane, London E. do solemnly and sincerely declare that Bessie Hoffman is my daughter. She was born of April 1903 at [the] Ploonsk, Russian Poland." The document is signed with a cross.

Bessie, whose father was Shmuel Meir Hoffman, was the eldest of four children – a brother Nat and two sisters Lily and Sarah (Soorie) who would be born in the East End. Lily went on to marry Jack Kyiet while Sarah married Joe Kutner who went into the paint business. Brother Nat turned out to be the rebel of the family; he changed his name from Hoffman to the more anglicised Kenton, much to the annoyance of the family.

Those were the days when incongruities often arose when recording the birth of a child. Confusion surfaced when different family members were asked to register the names of children. Poor literacy and no standard transliteration of Jewish names made it difficult, with the result that many names were spelt phonetically and variations of spelling within families were not uncommon.

There were many family stories. Uncle Dave had once claimed to see a ghost in the house in Severne Street. His father Isaac told him that if he ever saw the ghost again he should walk towards it and confront the phantom and it would disappear. It was later surmised that the house had been built over an old plague-pit, but this was all conjecture. Leslie's grandmother Sarah, being a bit of a psychic herself, once had her palm read and was accurately informed that she would lead a hard life but would reach old age and have lots of children. However, given that this applied to many women from that period, the revelation should have come as no great surprise.

The Jewish East End was a self-contained neighbourhood with community life focused on Wentworth Street, or The Lane, which echoed with the activities and cries of the Yiddish-speaking hawkers and traders. The day-to-day ebb and flow of life moved at a measured pace. East End Jewry led an extremely religious life and synagogues were usually packed to capacity, although Friday evening services were often prolonged by drawn-out, laborious sermons often demanding congregants to listen for two hours or more.

Many immigrants found employment locally, mostly in the clothing industry which at the turn of the 20th century consisted of small sweat-shops where there was a group of skilled and unskilled workers manufacturing men's and ladies' coats and skirts. Depending on the size of the businesses, owners would often employ up to ten workers at a time who were kept active for long hours in cramped and unhealthy environments. Without fresh air, exercise and regular meals these sweatshops proved to be an ideal breeding ground for tuberculosis and other diseases prevalent at that time.

While the clothing industry dominated the East End, other people found employment as market traders and shopkeepers. But one thing was assured – if there were Jewish families in the neighbourhood then there would be a demand for one commodity that has always interested them, namely food, because the Jews loved to eat.

Food became a major priority and the poorest families were never allowed to go hungry. The women could make a meal out of the cheapest cuts of meat, fish and fowl. Black bread and fresh herrings – mostly salted, others marinated, some chopped and mixed with apples and grated boiled eggs – were inexpensive to buy, full of nutrition and a family favourite. Housewives could buy the herrings from a barrel and schmaltz herrings held a particular appeal in most Jewish households. These were prepared by smoking young fat spring herrings using a process created by Dutch fishermen. Soups, such as green lentil broth with added meat and potatoes, were a wholesome, tasty dish and there was always the Jewish universal panacea for all ailments – chicken soup with barley. Subsequently there was a huge demand and Jewish grocery stores, bagel bakeries, poultry, butcher shops and fish huts sprang up like wild mushrooms.

EARLY BOYHOOD

With their families living next door to each other it was inevitable that Harry and Bessie, who grew up together, became soul-mates. It came as no surprise when the couple became engaged and eventually married. No *shadkhan* (matchmaker) was needed to find these two life-long partners and blessings were showered on the couple from both families.

Their wedding took place on 20 February 1923 in the Grove Street Synagogue, very close to Severne Street. The wedding party was held in the upstairs banqueting hall of Silberstein's restaurant, just off Whitechapel Road, in a long, narrow hall with tables in front and people dancing the Hora in the space beyond.

Harry and Bessie's wedding, 20 February 1923

Bessie and Harry's wedding -
all the family together

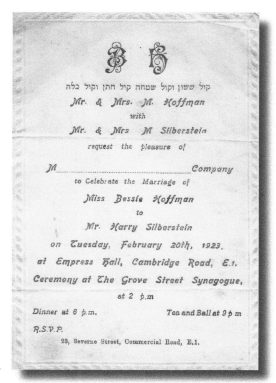

The wedding invitation

Harry, Bessie and baby
Leslie, December 1925

In 1926, fifteen months after Leslie was born, Bessie gave birth to a daughter whom they named Gilda, and roughly eighteen months later another son, Stanley, appeared adding to the growing family unit. In those days sex education was hardly spoken about – in fact in some homes it was a strictly taboo subject and not up for discussion. A family joke was that with the quick succession of children after her marriage it suddenly dawned on naive Bessie what had 'caused it', something she'd never considered.

Leslie, Gilda and Stanley were amongst the first grandchildren of a rather large family and so there was plenty of love to go around. All of the children were adored by their parents but it was Leslie who was always regarded as 'the favoured one', which surprisingly never translated into any sibling rivalry, at least not according to outsiders.

Stanley, always looked upon as the baby of the family, thrived in the company of his older brother and sister and the children soon became very close. There were many happy memories of playing

Family seaside holiday
1932. Harry, Stanley,
Gilda, Leslie and Bessie

together through jolly jaunts in municipal parks. Leslie recalls it was
'always summer', comprising an idyllic childhood with lots of
freedom, buttercups and May blossom, and the thrill of running wild
in nearby parkland and feeling bold and liberated.

One day the siblings were having a great game of tumbling and
rolling in the park's green grass when they found themselves observed
by a young boy who longed to join in. Stanley was having none of it
and, turning around, sent the youngster away with a flea in his ear.
The youngest child had become quite territorial; this was his club
where only close kith and kin were allowed membership.

On those carefree days out the children came across lots of horses
and carts and, because Harry was a
keen gardener, Leslie knew he could
make a bob or two selling horse
manure for gardens. Showing an
early sign of his future entrepreneurial flair, he and Gilda
followed the horses with a supply
of sacks. As the youngest, Stanley
was instructed to pick up the
droppings by hand. He dutifully
obeyed, but is fondly remembered
for saying afterwards: "I didn't
realise that *that* was manure."

Leslie and
Gilda at the
seaside

In the light of the present-day fearful mind-set it is hard to believe that, at that moment in time, children were actually encouraged to play outside either on their own or with friends and in the summer months allowed to stay there long into dusk. As far as the children were concerned they were growing up and having the time of their lives. The trio enjoyed the open air and more often than not, without being conscious of any danger, would go on walkabouts, loving nothing better than wandering about in woods and parks, exploring their neighbourhood and communing with nature.

On two occasions at least Gilda went so far out that she got lost and had to be brought home by a policeman. Another time, Leslie also disappeared and after two or three hours Bessie and Harry became worried. Aged nine, Leslie had always wanted to visit the Science Museum and his parents had promised that someday they would take him there, but this pledge was never redeemed. Nevertheless, when the wanderer finally returned, his much relieved mother asked him to explain his disappearance. "I went to the Science Museum", he replied. Bessie's eyebrows arched to heaven. "The Science Museum?" she asked in exasperation. The Science Museum was a long way from home, "How on earth did you get there?" But her initial inclination to continue scolding turned into astonishment when Leslie started to reel off a list of all the wonderful things he had seen during his time in the museum, describing in minute detail his ride by public transport to get there and producing the ticket as evidence.

This was an early indication of how, if Leslie wanted to do something, go somewhere or achieve anything then nothing on earth would faze or prevent him from fulfilling his yearning. His mother called him *ferbrent* which in Yiddish meant that if Leslie wanted something he "burned" to have it immediately – things could not be put off till tomorrow.

For a short time Gilda was a girl guide and Leslie went into the scout movement. The eldest child liked nothing better than to try his hand at anything on offer, always eager to investigate new territory and explore fresh fields and to confirm that he'd been there, done that, and was able to add another tick to his long list of fulfilled wishes.

He also liked to read the popular boys' comic papers of the day and enthusiastically built up a collection of the Beano and the Dandy which he would store in a corner of his bedroom, much to the annoyance of Bessie who thought comics were a distraction, rather inconsequential and not the sort of literature she wanted her children to peruse. Bessie had strict house rules. She wouldn't let Gilda read romantic fiction, dismissing it as badly written and rubbish. "What will that teach you about life?", she asked. Anything remotely 'racy' would be frowned upon and quickly consigned to the rubbish bin.

But not everything was suffused with a golden light at that time. One of Leslie's earliest memories came as the result of the distress he felt after losing his paternal grandfather in 1935. This was an early brush with family bereavement and he felt the loss deeply and was forlorn and hopelessly dejected for some time afterwards.

His father's mother, Sarah, who died in 1951, eventually went to live with her son Ashy who had moved to Manchester and who survived through the dark days of the gathering storm which in due course led to a second world war. Leslie drew much comfort from the knowledge that she was out of harm's way and had been kept safe and sound.

Family life had been, and continued to be, a priority. Bessie, a proud and intelligent woman, was a wonderful cook who stayed mainly with traditional food, but with a keen interest in the values of healthy eating. She was eager to see her family receive a nutritious and well-balanced diet and some foods were forbidden, particularly that with high fat content – which wasn't easy considering the ingredients that went into Jewish cuisine.

For example, Bessie wouldn't let her children eat fried chips, telling them that fried food wasn't particularly good for their digestive system or heart arteries. For that era that was quite advanced thinking, given that most Jewish households were feasting on blintzes, latkes, doughnuts and pieces of fish all deep-fried in oil, but starved of medical health warnings and information. This was in complete contrast to *bobba* Sarah whose first words as she placed on the table heaped plates full of home-cooked food dripping in fat and oil "*Ess, ess, ess*, children, strength comes from eating, so eat, eat, eat."

Everything in Bessie's meticulously clean kitchen was home-made. Quite often she ordered her daughter Gilda to drink boiled cabbage water as part of her evening meal. "Drink this", she would instruct, "it's good for you." She also realised the richly nutritional benefits of beetroot, whether raw, pickled or made into a delicious ruby-red borsht, a soup she would often thicken with beaten eggs. Another favourite was cabbage borsht, but this was made with slices of brisket and a marrow bone which turned the dish into a delicious winter meal-in-one.

The Silver home was a cultural haven – there were always books to read and, with Harry's great love of classical music, a stack of shellac records to play on his much prized mahogany-cased gramophone. Discussion, music, debate and politics were high on the Silver household agenda. Music had been ingrained into the family; Uncle Dave had played drums with a band in the 1930s and Uncle Ashy was adept at the Jew's harp. Even Aunt Hannah was a proficient pianist and Leslie himself was to endure endless hours of learning to play the violin.

Bessie was ambitious and eager for her children to receive schooling that would teach them to do well in the world. She longed for them to have a university education and study to be lawyers or doctors, eagerly egging them on to become 'proper professionals.'

Harry and Bessie had a perfect relationship albeit sometimes based on conflicting values. He was always very level-headed while Bessie was more assertive and over-riding. During arguments, Harry would often throw in the towel, if for no other reason than just to have a bit of peace and quiet. Leslie and his mother also had many differences of opinion; both were strong-willed and more often than not Leslie, purposeful and focussed, refused to be told what to do and often insisted on having the last word.

As a small child Leslie and his two siblings looked forward to staying with their grandparents in Severne Street and to the lively preparation leading up to the Sabbath. The smell of cooking and baking was evident from early Thursday morning. The focus of activity was always food, exemplified by the big cooking range which was fired by a roaring coal fire. Something delicious was constantly cooking slowly on the hob or in the oven – a feast of culinary delights. As long as there was warmth inside the home and food on the table, this was the best of all possible worlds.

Grandma Sarah would hustle and bustle around the house, eventually revealing the sparkling white linen table cloth from the top drawer of the dresser which she produced with a flourish like a music-hall magician suddenly producing a rabbit out of a hat. She painstakingly laid out the cloth on the solid wooden table until every crease was smoothed away and every corner corresponded in perfect symmetry.

The candlesticks, treasured possessions lovingly brought from the old country by her forebears, would be polished yet again. The pure white candles would be placed on a salver together with the candlesticks in readiness for the great moment when they would be kindled late afternoon to herald in the Sabbath. There would also be wine and silver drinking cups and a round *challah* bread under an embroidered *challa* cloth. Later that evening there would be *kiddush*, the ceremony of reciting prayers and blessings over a cup of wine at the commencement of Sabbath. The belief behind *kiddush* is that holy time must be differentiated from irreligious time by proclaiming its holiness.

Apart from her maternal, religious and domestic observance, fuelled by a steely resolution, Sarah, assisted by one of her sons, would also be occupied by carrying in pails of water which she obtained from the back yard, making certain the supply would last the family over the long 24-hour period of the Sabbath.

One of her idiosyncrasies was to have fresh flowers on the Friday night table which she always placed in a valued cut-glass vase. Flowers were important to her and sometimes when strapped for cash she even pawned an odd item of clothing to enable her to purchase a small floral addition to her Sabbath table.

Occasionally during the meal a heated debate would erupt; the subject was nearly always political since, after all, what else was there to argue about. Sarah was aware that things could easily get out of hand. As a consequence, she would stand up defiantly and, having lifted the vase of flowers off the table, would escort it to a safer place, just in case it was knocked over. Yelling over the disagreement she would raise her fist in the air and plead, "*Sheket bevakashah* (Quiet, please!) – be careful of my flower vase."

The weekend included hours of religious observance involving the whole family. The municipal bathhouse was situated down the street and hot baths were eagerly taken. Fresh, cleanly laundered clothes were set out at home with shoes buffed to a gleaming patina.

Young Leslie, approaching Bar Mitzvah age, was often taken to the nearby synagogue on Friday night as well as Sabbath morning by his paternal *zayda.* It was a time he particularly enjoyed – a time when the community came together to pray, gossip, catch-up on news, talk, pray again and talk some more.

When the Saturday synagogue service was over and the congregants walked together on the way back home, Leslie, hand in hand with his beloved *zayda,* would pop into the local bakery to collect the huge *cholent* which had been bubbling in the oven overnight. Cholent was a traditional Sabbath dish which Sarah and Bessie had previously made in a huge brown *schissel* (earthenware pot) and which had been cooked to golden perfection. The recipe, brought over from the *shtetls* (villages) of Eastern Europe, favoured being cooked slowly and served as the main course for the Sabbath luncheon. The main ingredients were meat on the bone, beans, onions and potatoes – a wholesome, economical and nourishing dish for a hungry family.

On Saturday evenings in the East End of the early thirties, social activity in the community spilled out onto the pavements of nearby Whitechapel Road as families celebrated the close of the Sabbath with the Saturday walk. As members of the neighbourhood passed each other in the street, families would greet each other with the customary nod and a tiding to "have a good week." A *seudah shlishit,* Hebrew for third meal, was always eaten on Sabbath. Tradition dictated that three meals had to be eaten on Sabbath to make a distinction between Saturday and the rest of the week. This extra third meal was always added later on Saturday afternoon and, although not as weighty as the second meal, mostly consisted of *challah* (bread), hard-boiled eggs, herrings (pickled, soused or chopped) and pieces of fried and *gefulte* (chopped and boiled) fish.

Fish was a staple diet in most Jewish households, and a food that could be prepared and cooked prior to the Sabbath and served cold on the holiest day of the week. The ritual on the New Year festival (Rosh Hashanah), for example, involves symbolically casting away sins into a stream which contains fish so they can carry the sins away to the sea. Fish are especially suitable for this task because their eyes are always open and being covered by water they are not subject to *ayin hara,* the evil eye.

≈ ≈ ≈

The clothing and tailoring industries were the only trades the families knew, so when Harry left school on the cusp of his teenage years he became a tailor to a firm of clothiers, eventually moving on to work in Walthamstow in the north east of London. When he found difficulty obtaining employment during the years of the Depression he decided to open a market stall in Ridley Road. Although the market was renowned for retail food it also housed a few general stalls and a friend gave Harry some shellac records to sell, but the only one that ever sold satisfactorily was Al Jolson's trendy Sonny Boy from the first talking movie The Jazz Singer which was all the rage. As a five-year-old in the winter of 1930, Leslie's job was to take a little tin can filled with hot soup or tea and some sandwiches to Harry, who secretly hated every minute of market life. On the other hand, every time he played the Jolson record a crowd assembled, the women dabbing their eyes on their aprons at the poignant lyrics and Harry's takings swelled.

When Leslie was ten, in 1935, the family made quite a dramatic relocation from Waterloo Road to Victoria Park and the suburb of Cambridge Heath. In his own simple way Harry was a man of ambition and had a secret dream. He had for a long time hankered to launch his own tailoring business and had come across a large yard with a garage and a forecourt big enough to park five cars. There was also a small house adjoining the land. It was an ideal accommodation which he felt comfortable renting and it was an area he had long admired, and so had the children after frequent visits to the park. Few people had cars, and that included Harry, but the ones that did lived in houses without the added luxury of a garage. He saw a way of utilising the garage space and sub-let it out to local car-owners.

Above the garage there was a substantial wooden-floored area which Harry turned into a workshop. It was there he employed his father as a presser and his two brothers Joe and Dave, as tailors, before bringing in his sisters Betty, the eldest, and Hannah, the youngest, as well as Anne, the family's adopted daughter, as machinists and under-pressers. The Silver family was now in business, and that made a huge difference to the family income. Harry continued to provide a good living for his family, even acquiring a brand new telephone and a wireless which took pride of place in the front room. However, modern technology knew no bounds and Harry cleverly wired an extension into the kitchen so Bessie could hear the wireless as she cooked and baked.

With Harry to supervise the firm, which now had a workforce of seven making ladies' garments, the business was given extra kudos by the patronage of the renowned department store Bourne and Hollingsworth. The store, an imposing edifice built in 1894 and remodelled in 1928 in art deco style, was situated at the corner of Oxford Street and

Leslie aged about 10 years old

Berners Street. This area was the cornerstone of the city's retail emporia and it was a great feather in Harry's cap to have orders pouring in on a regular basis. Only a plaque outside announcing 'under Royal patronage' could have surpassed that honour. Harry had been recommended to the firm by a tailoring friend after B&H had started to contract local tailors to do alterations for their ladies' clothing department.

But there was trouble ahead which manifested itself when, in the late 1930s, Harry's business started to take a plunge. This was partly because trade in general had started to decline but mainly because Bourne and Hollingsworth put pressure on Harry and argued about prices, resulting in no further orders. Not one for waiting around to see if things improved, Harry thought it was an ideal time to sell up and make a fresh start. If the business was ailing then Harry's philosophy was not to mope about, but to move on to pastures new.

Without waiting for the grass to grow under his feet he closed down the business and found employment as a manager, pattern cutter and designer with a firm called Stanley Morrie, and uprooted the family from Cambridge Heath to new domestic arrangements. Harry had managed to accrue some savings and always dreamt of a house with a garden. Fortunately he came across, and then rented, a residence in Charter Avenue in Walthamstow where he was to spend many happy hours working in the sizeable grounds.

The family joined the Highams Park Hebrew Congregation and it was at the Marlborough Road Synagogue that Leslie read a portion of the law at his Bar Mitzvah on Saturday, 7 May 1938. To commemorate the occasion his parents pulled out all the stops and made a reception, dinner, buffet and ball the following day at Stern's Hotel in Mansell Street, Aldgate. In a tight new suit and his thick black hair smoothed down with brilliantine, Leslie stood up and made a short speech in appreciation of his family's support – this was the first time he had spoken in public and he felt very grown up as nearby guests were hushed to listen to the Bar Mitzvah boy.

Leslie's Bar Mitzvah 1938. Harry, Bessie, Leslie, with Gilda and Stanley in front

בר מצוה

Mr. & Mrs. H. Silver

request the pleasure of the company of

----

to celebrate the Confirmation of their son

Leslie

who will read a portion of the Law at the

Marlborough Road Synagogue, Highams Park

on Saturday, May 7th, 1938.

Reception at 7.30 p.m.

Dinner at 8.   Buffet & Ball at 9.30

on Sunday, May 8th,

at Stern's Hotel, 3 & 5, Mansell Street, Aldgate, E. 1

48, Charter Avenue,   *R. S. V. P.*
Walthamstow, E. 17   *on or before May 1st.*

Invitation to Leslie's
Bar Mitzvah

Father and son enjoying
the Bar Mitzvah

≈ ≈ ≈

The family was shaken to its very foundations when, a year before the outbreak of war, Uncle Ashy announced to all and sundry that he and his wife Sarah were leaving the East End and moving to Manchester. Summoned to hear the declaration in the front parlour, family members listened pale-faced and confused as Ashy told them he had to think about his future. Wanting a better life for himself, the eldest son informed them that he had found work in Lancashire as a tailor in the clothing industry.

Leslie's immigrant grandparents spoke not one word of English, choosing instead to converse in Yiddish – and this was the patois Harry and Bessie preferred to use when they didn't want the children to understand their private conversations. On the other hand, their body language and heated discussions, even in a foreign language, spoke volumes. As Ashy broke the news and tried to offer some sort of reasonable explanation, the family listened with shock and disbelief. "Manchester?", they asked one another, "why Manchester?", as if the famous industrial city was situated in some far distant land – as in a sense it was for people who had never ventured north of London.

It was true that the furthest any of the family had travelled was nearby Stepney Green. This was a family happiest in its own environment where everything and everyone was familiar – they didn't take too heartily to change. No matter how Ashy reasoned with them the family could not be pacified. As far as his parents were concerned this was a contravention of the old world order by the young.

But the times were shifting and the name Silverstein had become anglicized to Silver and was changed by deed poll on 18 August 1938 by Bessie and Harry for a fee of ten shillings, with the rest of the family soon following suit. The Silver dynasty en masse soon emerged ready to tackle modern-day life head on.

Two

1939 - 1947

IF TRUTH BE TOLD, LESLIE always thought he was a great disappointment to his parents. His mother had already made clear her thoughts on education. Bessie wanted to have a son who had a reasonable education so he could enjoy a better standard of living than his parents had. So she pushed him to succeed, especially in his examinations. Although Leslie was intelligent he was not a scholar and had difficulty focussing on lessons and keeping up with other pupils. This served to hold back his progress and he was to admit many years later that he felt 'an absolute failure' who had no expectations of success.

This was certainly confirmed by his teachers who were uniformly gloomy. Bessie was called to the school and was told by one teacher that the sooner Leslie left school and found employment the better. "I'm sorry to say, Mrs Silver, he will never amount to much."

Not even, it seems, as a musician. In those days the great violinist Yehuda Menuhin was a prime example of an ideal young teenage role model for Jewish children. Every Jewish mother wanted her son to be a Menuhin and for some months Leslie, to please his mother, was even persuaded to take violin lessons. That proved to be rather painful for anyone in earshot and happily did not last long, to the gratitude of family, neighbours, dogs and cats and young Leslie himself. He was much happier playing a game of soccer with the kids in the street.

The 1918 Fisher Act after the Great War brought in a standard leaving age for all children of fourteen years, although some schools did allow pupils to leave aged twelve. The 1936 Education Act raised the school leaving age to fifteen but empowered LEAs to issue employment certificates to allow 14-year-olds to work rather than attend school in certain circumstances, especially where a family would suffer exceptional hardship if the child did not work. When Leslie left school at Easter 1939, aged fourteen, he could read, write and had mastered arithmetic, up to a point, and that was the extent of his education. It was evident that Leslie would soon make working life his university.

POLITICS AND THE WORLD OF WORK

The political inclination in the East End was mostly left wing. The Spanish Civil War (fought from 1936 to 1939 between the Republicans loyal to the established Spanish Republic, and the Nationalists, a rebel group led by General Franco) had started and the emergence of fascism was making its unsettling presence known.

It was the rise of Sir Oswald Mosley that led many to the political left in England and to enrol in the ever-growing Communist party. Jews were constantly being attacked and the Silver family, amongst many others, reacted with horror and condemnation. Mosley's East End attacks continued and he and his notorious Blackshirts paraded through the streets beating elderly Jews and picking on young boys on the way home from *cheder* (Hebrew school).

Mosley had built up a reputation as a public speaker immersed in political rhetoric that swayed some of his listeners to follow his abhorrent views. The liberal Westminster Gazette once wrote that Mosley was "the most polished literary speaker in the Commons. Words flow from him in graceful epigrammatic phrases that have a sting in them for the government and the Conservatives. To listen to him is an education in the English language and also in the art of delicate, but deadly, repartee."

Mosley was a scion of an old landed family. In 1922, he had left the Conservative party to become an Independent and two years later joined the Labour party. In 1930, Mosley had made a bold bid for political advancement within the Labour party. When Labour won the 1929 general election he was appointed merely to the post of Chancellor of the Duchy of Lancaster, but was given responsibility for solving the unemployment problem. Finding his radical proposals blocked, he put forward a scheme in the Mosley Memorandum which called for high tariffs to protect British industries from foreign imports and for state nationalisation of the main industries, as well as a programme for public works to tackle unemployment. However, this was rejected by the cabinet and in May 1930 he resigned from his ministerial position.

In 1931, he united his New Party, along with earlier-formed fascist groups, into the British Union of Fascists and aligned the ideological identity of his movement with those of Mussolini in Italy and Hitler in Germany.

For their part, the Silver family became fiercely political and ardently associated with the Communist party. In 1936, Leslie, just eleven years old, had participated in what turned out to be one of the major pre-war anti-fascist rallies, when Mosley and his Blackshirts attempted another walk through the East End. This march, held on 4 October 1936, became better known as the Battle of Cable Street. Harry had insisted that the young lad go with him to observe the protest. This was a clash between the Metropolitan Police, who were on duty to supervise a march by the British Union of Fascists (BUF) led by Mosley, and anti-fascist protestors including local Jewish residents, activists, socialists, anarchists, Irish and communist groups. It was to pan out as a defining moment in history.

Both the Labour party and the Board of Deputies of British Jews denounced the march as anti-semitic and urged Jewish people to stay away. The Communist party, under the leadership of Phil Piratin, led the opposition forces. Piratin's role was widely recognised by local people and the following year he became the first Communist to be elected to Stepney Borough Council, leading to his election as a Communist MP for Mile End in 1945.

Ignoring the warnings of danger, the Jewish community turned out in force to oppose the march. The anti-fascist groups had built road blocks and barricades in an attempt to prevent the march from taking place. The barricades were constructed near the junction with Christian Street towards the west end of the street, and an estimated 100,000 anti-fascists demonstrators turned out. They were to be confronted by a 6,000 strong police force who attempted to clear the road to permit the march, involving nearly 3,000 fascists, to proceed. But the demonstrators were having none of it and Leslie witnessed them fighting back with sticks, rocks and anything else they could get their hands on – even the heavy iron poker that rested on many a fireplace inglenook was used as a weapon. He remembered chair legs, which had been sawn off from old furniture, being hurled into the air and household rubbish raining down like a frantic ticker-tape reception. In some cases, extreme measures were taken when the contents of bedroom chamber pots and commodes were thrown at the police by Jewish housewives.

With no other option, Mosley capitulated and agreed to abandon the protest march and the BUF marchers were disbanded and told to move to Hyde Park instead. The memory of the event stayed forever in Leslie's mind and, deeply rooted in his consciousness, proved to be the motivating factor that prompted him to join the RAF years later to continue the fight against fascism. The commemorative Dock Street plaque, with the slogan 'They Shall Not Pass', records how the people of East London rallied to Cable Street to force back the march of the Blackshirts through the streets of the East End.

Although there was widespread poverty, the East End continued to plant the seeds and provide inspiration for the success of many a young person's later life. Saying goodbye to school in 1939 was a blessed relief for Leslie. He was being constantly told he was not an academic and found it difficult to focus and listen to what was being taught. He had two things on his mind – politics and football.

Harry, through his employment at nearby tailoring business Stanley Morrie, where he was working as junior manager, soon found an opening for Leslie. Harry secretly worried about what his son's future would be. One thing was certain, his eldest son needed to be taught a trade. The factory was owned by two tailors and was situated near Wentworth Street, known as Petticoat Lane, and in close proximity to Blooms kosher restaurant. Outside the restaurant was to be found the famous bagel lady who held a big basket full of freshly baked bagels and whose street cry of "three-a-penny-bagels" was as familiar a sound as Bow Bells.

On his first day at his new job, Leslie sat in a row of some thirty machinists in a steamy room learning how to operate a sewing machine – a more incongruous sight could not be found. Over six feet tall and with a well-built frame, Leslie towered above the other machinists and stood out like a sore thumb. Sitting for long spells at a time hunched over a sewing machine brought its own hazards, particularly bad posture, muscle tension and cramp and because of his physical size Leslie was not immune.

It was early spring, very warm and flies were buzzing everywhere. The room was thick with dust and the windows clouded with dirt. As one of his first tasks Leslie received instruction on how to sew up the seams of sleeves which he managed to execute with great dexterity. Later on he was given the opportunity to have a go at becoming a cutter – cutting the fabric according to patterns, which he did with less enthusiasm and success. Leslie was instructed to cut around the outline to eventually make a garment. Layers of fabric were put down on a large table and the pattern placed over one of them. Cutting was a precise art that Harry possessed in spades. Somehow his son, all-fingers-and-thumbs, managed to cut the cloth differently for each design. It was not a pretty sight and confirmation, if confirmation was needed, that cutting was not to be Leslie's forte.

Nevertheless, with nothing else on the horizon it appeared that this was the only industry that could open doors to Leslie's future livelihood. However, the bubble burst when foreman Alec, a Russian Jew who taught Leslie to use a sewing machine, came across to him at 6pm at the end of a day's work. Nodding his head very slowly and wisely he said quietly: "Leslie, if you're a good boy and you work very hard, in forty years time you might be half as good as your father."

The jocular put-down pulled Leslie up short; the idea of staying in the clothing industry for four decades not merely disheartened him but sent alarm bells ringing – this was the straw that broke the camel's back and he had to make his escape. He disliked the drudgery and monotony that the trade was going to offer him and, as someone who never could sit still for more than two minutes, Leslie was inwardly dreading a working life of complete and utter boredom. Put simply he realised that the solution rested with him, and only him, to work out larger plans to find a way out. Surely, he thought, there was something else he was better suited to do. Whatever he chose for the years ahead he had to get away from the clothing trade.

≈ ≈ ≈

War was imminent and during the period known as the phoney war, Leslie and Gilda were evacuated to Wellingborough, but were soon sent back home when nothing happened. This was a phase marked by a lack of major military operations by the Western Allies against the German Reich. Expecting the 'real war' to start at any time, Harry had already built an air-raid shelter in the bottom of the garden at Charter Avenue. When war was declared on 3 September 1939 and the blitz eventually started, it exceeded all expectations – it was nothing short of horrific. The year 1940 was Britain's first full year of war and the country's very existence was being threatened. Although Churchill was to declare this to be 'the country's finest hour', defeat and occupation were real possibilities. After failing to crush the RAF in the Battle of Britain, the Luftwaffe turned its attention to night bombing raids against London and other cities. The blitz was intended to cause as much disruption as possible and Hitler's wish was to bring production to a grinding halt and so destroy the country's economy – it was also focused on breaking the morale of the British people.

Air raids became heavier and during August 1940 and the months that followed over 43,000 civilians were killed. Among the first bombs to drop in the East End one was to hit the tailoring factory of Stanley Morrie – no one was injured but the owners decided they had to get out of London. The tailoring firm had already acquired a small showroom in Leeds, so the factory moved to Cross Stamford Street in Sheepscar where the business had already been established. The two partners transformed the showroom into a workshop and production recommenced.

Harry, with the prospect of future managerial employment in Leeds at Stanley Morrie, also decided to escape the London bombing. In December 1940 he travelled to Leeds and rented a house for ten shillings a week at 30 Easterly Avenue in the district of Harehills, eventually bringing all the family to Yorkshire to stay, perhaps for just six months or so or at least until the war was over.

Leeds was already the epicentre of the British clothing industry and with the advancement of mass production, new machinery, better conditions and the chance to be taught the trade and earn decent money, many young men and women were entering the industry. Leslie went to work for a short time in the dreaded cutting department of the new Stanley Morrie factory which he disliked intensely. However, it was employment and he was thankful to be earning some wages in very difficult times.

Apart from Mosley there was now Hitler to contend with and Leslie became more left-wing than ever. He felt that neither the Labour nor Conservative parties were fighting the fascists so inevitably he joined the Young Communist League (YCL) at 51 Francis Street in Chapeltown, which was, he thought, a natural and logical progression. It was a challenging time for Leslie. As there was no school to attend there were no school pals. He was a boisterous East-Ender in Yorkshire who liked a good argument, especially if it was political, and he liked to be tested. As a result, most of his friends and acquaintances were from the YCL.

He become quite active in the League, and was soon offered a job as shop assistant in the organisation's bookshop in Woodhouse Lane, selling mostly political and left-wing literature. Surrounded by books, creative writing and some radical political propaganda, young Leslie was in his element. After working in the noisy clothing industry he enjoyed the peace and quiet that the shop offered, and took pleasure in chatting to like-minded people and particularly reading up on politics. As a full-time employee of the CP bookshop, Leslie came to know Bert Ramelson and his first wife Marion very well. In fact as the bookshop administrator, it was Leslie's job to report to him. Ramelson was an expert pamphleteer and his literary contributions to the League pamphlets were well thought out and proficiently executed. Leslie knew also of his gift of oratory as Ramelson's protest speeches on the steps of Leeds Town Hall were legendary.

Ramelson, whose real name was Baruch Rahmilevich Mendelson, was born in the Ukraine on 22 March 1910, the sixth of seven children of a Jewish family in Cherkassy. His father, Jacob, was a Talmudic scholar while his mother ran a corner shop, inherited from her father, and in which the family resided in the rooms above. Ramelson spoke Yiddish and Hebrew fluently, although many people found him difficult to cope with, partly because of his extremely loud and dominant voice. One didn't need a microphone when he was around. In 1922 his family had emigrated to Canada where an uncle was a successful fur trader and, after winning a scholarship to the University of Alberta, he achieved first class honours in law. After completing his Articles he left to join a Kibbutz in Palestine and, after briefly returning to Canada, he left again to fight in the Spanish Civil War. In 1939, he settled in Britain and for a short time was a trainee manager at Marks and Spencer, but post-war he became acting full-time secretary to the Leeds branch of the Communist party, holding the position from 1946 to 1953. He encouraged political activism within the Yorkshire mining community, working regularly with the National Union of Mineworkers.

There was wide support in the Jewish community for the Communist party at all income levels, although the main support came from the working class and some professionals and academics. Leslie, young and idealistic, was carried along with left-wing political passion and he enjoyed chatting with Ramelson on quite a few occasions.

Ramelson told him that the bare bones of Marxism were all about three elements – the State, the Class and the Party – and it was the relationship between those three factors that turned out to be one of Ramelson's many legacies. But with the luxury of hindsight, and many years later, Leslie came to regret his support for the Communist party. To Leslie, the party was the only one that appeared to be doing anything about standing up to the fascists. He felt that communism sounded 'all right at the time', but it was to prove, in retrospect, an ideology that never really worked. "We were obviously so wrong", he was to confess to a 1998 after-dinner audience. "Our political fervour, our desire to beat the fascists through supporting the communists was wrong. It was a mistake and beyond comprehension how my generation could have been so misguided." This then was definitely a period of his life that Leslie came to regret.

LESLIE GOES TO WAR

There were four reasons why Leslie volunteered for the air force when he was seventeen – he was British, Jewish and a communist and he wanted to fly.

Because the war was not short-lived the family had decided to settle in Leeds. They had a home, employment and, compared to the East End, felt reasonably safe. Because of his lack of education Leslie didn't hold out much hope of becoming a pilot. However, he had good eye-sight and an enthusiasm that was engaging. Indeed this was recognised when he went before the RAF panel of officers in 1942 who were impressed with his burning commitment. They told him that without an education, which they regarded as a sure passport to success, there was no way they would consider him to be a pilot or navigator. Pilots had to be well-informed. Nevertheless, Leslie was more than ready to join the services and the teenager wanted desperately to fly and to travel.

At that time in 1942 the RAF was becoming short of crews and losing a lot of planes. They needed extra flight engineers and in his interview they asked him if he knew anything about engineering. An officer then held a baffling object up in the air and asked Leslie to identify it. The teenager said that he didn't know what it was. The officer told him it was a micrometer and Leslie replied: "It must be a different model from the ones I have seen."

He was tested further on the standard of his ability to absorb knowledge as an air gunner or a flight engineer. This time he knew most of the answers but he had absolutely no concept whatsoever of what made an engine work. When Leslie was ultimately made a flight engineer he was surprised, honoured and excited. He was sent to St Athans military base in Wales for a 26-week course with an exam taking place at lunchtime every Friday. It was a simple system of

The six month training course to be a flight engineer at St Athans, South Wales, 1943.
Leslie is second from right on the back row

teaching where failure was not tolerated. If that happened then apprentices were put back a week – and because Leslie was anxious to qualify he made sure he knew the answers and did not fail. As a result, at the end of the course, this 'uneducated, unqualified clothing worker' was trained to be a competent and valued member of a bomber command crew.

Many years later, Leslie argued that credit was due not only to the youth of his generation, but to those in the RAF who took on replacement crews, containing men from all walks of life, at a time when their country needed them the most. As Leslie affirms, "they recognised that the country was producing four-engine bombers for the first time and, of course, there were no people trained to handle them. They were being knocked out of the skies like nobody's business and they had to produce replacement crews, and quickly, so they took complete novices, like me, fed them into the sausage machine and the end product was a stream of competent members of air crew who were able to deliver the goods."

As airplanes became larger they required more engines and offered more sophisticated systems to operate. The amount of work assigned to pilots became too much during critical parts of the flight, most notably on takeoffs and landings. As a consequence, in order to monitor the engines and other flight systems, the position of flight engineer was created. Needless to say, Leslie did not actually fly the plane, which he would dearly have loved to do, but his job as flight engineer was nonetheless just as important a role. He had his own specialised control panel allowing him to monitor and control various aircraft systems. He worked in close coordination with the pilot during all phases of the flight. His position was usually placed on the main flight deck just aft of the pilot and co-pilot. His role was often referred to as 'the engineer', much like a ship's engineer, who was primarily concerned with operation and monitoring. Leslie was often called upon to diagnose, and where possible rectify, any fault that may have arisen. And, along with the pilots, the technical engineers were also being instructed about the new four-engine bombers that were coming into service.

His job was continually to observe a screen of gauges, so he had to be thoroughly conversant with all the instruments. He had to test the fuel content in the tanks; confirm the pressurisation and air conditioning; check the hydraulics, electrics, ice and rain protection, oxygen, fire and overheat fortification and powered flying controls; and have an extensive knowledge of general aerodynamics. He also had to set and adjust engine power during takeoff, climb and cruise as well as on go-arounds or indeed at any time the pilot requested a specific power setting during the bombing approach phase.

Leslie's training was thorough and he was in his element, finding the instruction period to be an amazing experience. During the first week he was taught the rudiments of what an aircraft was all about and shown the various systems. There was a lot to absorb. Further training took place at RAF Dishforth in North Yorkshire where he was ultimately made a flight sergeant and gained his wings.

He initially served in 138 Squadron at Tempsford, which did low-level missions at about 400 feet. RAF Tempsford was located just over two miles to the north east of Sandy in Bedfordshire. It was perhaps the most secret airfield of the Second World War. It was so secret that even locals didn't realise what was going on there.

Although Leslie was part of bomber command his squadron, a special duty regiment at Tempsford, dropped spies and supplies

138 Squadron, Tempsford, August 1944. Leslie (right) flew 42 missions with them under the command of Captain Doug Lawrence

to the underground movement in France, Belgium, Holland and Poland. RAF Tempsford was put together so as to give overflying enemy aircraft the impression it was disused. However, just after dusk on moonlit nights either side of the full moon, planes from 138 and 161 Squadrons would take off on top secret missions to the heart of the war-torn continent. They were sent on bomber command operations – involving almost 250 operation hours – and flew by moonlight, and without lights, in order to identify drop zones and deliver the supplies and secret agents that would assist the resistance forces to liberate Europe. It was Churchill's big secret.

On one such mission, flying a Halifax bomber, Leslie's crew was ordered to take charge of four attractive young French girls who parachuted into France as secret agents. Leslie started to chat to one of them – a lovely girl with dark hair and flashing eyes. Speaking in a deep seductive voice, the spy sidled up to him and whispered "Leslie, just before I jump would you do me a huge favour and kiss me goodbye." Not one to refuse such an amorous request, Leslie acquiesced. "It will be my pleasure", he replied gallantly. When the time came for her to jump she turned round and said, "Wish me good luck", and putting her arm around his neck drew his face closer to her lips, planting a huge kiss and bidding him a seductive *Adieu, cheri*", before jumping.

Leslie was like a cat that got the cream, and licking his forefinger made a gesture of triumph in the air. His grin soon dispersed when, a few hours later, he realised he'd been duped and his dreams of becoming a spy fiction hero straight out of Eric Ambler had been thwarted – the glamorous spy had deftly removed his revolver!

After reporting the incident to his superiors he was warned that he could be subject to a court martial – but luckily he managed to get away with a severe reprimand.

≈ ≈ ≈

It was during his time in Tempsford that Leslie had to address some of the harsher realities of life when he was informed that his beloved grandmother, Hannah, had died. Returning briefly, in 1944, to the East End for the funeral, he was appalled to see his old stomping ground in such squalid condition. He hadn't realised what a privileged position he and his RAF colleagues had held, recalling how 'cosseted and mollycoddled' they had been from being served the best food and receiving top medication as well as given special consideration on many occasions.

On one occasion he came home on leave and his father, who was then working at Leeds clothiers Charles Sumrie, never one to display much emotion, showed a surprising concern for Leslie's welfare. "How are you doing, son" " his father enquired and Leslie replied that he was doing fine. There was a long pause and then his father asked how many missions he had flown. When Leslie replied "Forty-two", his father looked amazed. "Forty-two? My God!", he exclaimed. He paused for a moment before asking "And how many more have you got to do?"

It had never occurred to Leslie that family members who had been left at home were also suffering. He was just doing his job – he was young and foolish enough to think that he would be one of the lucky ones who would never be shot down. But in that moment he became aware of just how much anxiety parents and loved ones of those who served really endured.

In August 1944 Leslie had come to the end of his first tour. The thrill of being up in the air had given him the wings to fly personally; his self-esteem had risen considerably and Leslie felt that he could succeed in anything he put his mind to. He had already been engaged on numerous sorties so before he went on a second tour he was given a respite for six months. Harry received the news with delight. "Thank God for that", he said. "Look, Leslie, I'm taking a day off tomorrow, what do you say to you and I going out for a drink?" It was an historic moment; the first and last time in his life that Leslie went into a pub with his father. The family was by now living in Easterly Avenue, in the suburb of Roundhay, and Leslie remembers walking down to the local pub, the Fforde Green, in uniform – walking six-feet tall alongside a very proud father.

As the war in Europe dragged on, Leslie was moved to 291 Squadron which was created as an anti-aircraft co-operation unit. Formed at Hutton Cranswick in East Yorkshire in 1941, the squadron was equipped with Martinets and then Hurricanes and Hudsons to provide practice for the anti-aircraft defences in eastern England. One of their aims was to tow targets and conduct simulated attacks, which they did at Butlins holiday camp in Filey. The unit was also equipped for a short time with the Vultee A-31 Vengeance, an American dive bomber built by Vultee Aircraft.

This led to Leslie joining 356 Squadron based in India which had been sent to the Far East to help liberate the region from the Japanese. This short-lived, long-range bomber squadron, which operated during 1944 and 1945, was located at Salbani, Bengal and was equipped with the Consolidated Liberator, an American heavy bomber designed by Consolidated Aircraft of San Diego, California. The squadron was hard-hitting and determined and attacked Japanese bases in South-East Asia, planting mines outside enemy harbours. Leslie's first operation took place on 10 June 1945 when the squadron bombed Japanese troop concentrations. In July 1945, the squadron moved to the Cocos Islands, half way between Ceylon and Australia and due south of Sumatra and Java, initially to prepare and support the invasion of Malaya and to fight the Japanese. However, the end of the war came before the invasion could be carried out and the squadron performed supply-dropping and transport duties until it was disbanded in November 1945. One of these missions was being sent to Changi Jail in Singapore with supplies for the prisoners who had been left in a shocking condition.

By this time, Leslie had been made a senior Warrant Officer and put in charge of the bar in the Sergeant's Mess on the Cocos Islands – one of his many arduous wartime duties. It was in this capacity that Leslie was given his first lesson in entrepreneurship.

Leslie in a Liberator plane flying from the Cocos Islands to Malaysia in February 1943 (taken by a friend flying in another plane!)

The RAF had a very simple principle whereby every sergeant, flight-sergeant and warrant officer was allocated a bottle of whisky, gin and sherry every two-weeks at 7s 6d a bottle. If supplies were not used they were returned to the NAAFI, a credit note was issued and fresh supplies were offered. One day, Leslie and his crew were sent to Colombo and visiting a riverside bar asked the barman for a whisky which cost five rupees, the

On the Cocos Islands, August 1945

equivalent of 7s 6d. Leslie was horrified and said that on the Cocos he could get a whole bottle for that price, to which the barman replied: "Mister, you bring that bottle here and I'll pay you two-pounds for it."

It was an offer Leslie could hardly refuse. The next time Leslie and his crew were due to fly in was three weeks later but they had a number of dilemmas to address. In the first place, they had to fly the whisky to the military airport near Colombo. The solution was to remove their parachutes from their bags – reasoning that if you got into trouble over the ocean your parachute wouldn't be much use anyway – and to fill the bags with whisky bottles weighing much the same. Another dilemma was how to get the bottles of whisky out to the bar on the waterfront. Leslie decided to phone up the guard-house and to order a taxi on the pretext that he had hurt his knee and was unable to walk. By the time the taxi had arrived, Leslie and his pals had two full cases of whisky by way of luggage and these were placed in the boot of the car. When the taxi drew up to the main gates they were asked where they were heading. "We're going into Colombo," Leslie shouted from the back-seat. "Any luggage with you?" the guard enquired. "No luggage, officer", he called back. "Carry on through, then" came the reply.

In this manner, Leslie and his crew managed to smuggle forty bottles of whisky to the bar owner, selling each for two pounds a bottle. Leslie was to recount later that it was the best 7s 6d he was ever to spend in his entire life. The profits, together with the gratuity he received when demobilised from the RAF, came in very useful when Leslie was to be offered a business venture in the year ahead.

Of the 800,000 members in Bomber Command, some 200,000 were destined never to return. Leslie felt that his survival was down to sheer luck but at the same time he was deeply dismayed at how many of his good friends were killed. All through his life, Leslie felt an inner-pride at being part of a service that made a major contribution to helping save his country from invasion. That pride extended to having been part of an organisation that destroyed fascism.

ENTER ANITA

Whilst Leslie was serving in the Cocos Islands, he received a letter from England from a girl he had left behind, Anita Feddy, who lived in Trafford Terrace in Harehills.

The pair had gone out together casually since meeting at the Young Communist League in the early forties and had struck up, what Leslie always described as, 'a nice friendship.' One of the advantages of Bomber Command was that Leslie had plenty of leave and the couple used to frequent the Jubilee Hall in Savile Mount, which was the main community centre where young Jewish men and women socialised.

Afterwards, Leslie and Anita would often walk up Chapeltown Road to Cantor's fish and chip shop on the corner of Harehills Avenue. This venue also acted as a prominent setting for many young couples with romantic intent. Inside the shop was a back room with an area reserved for patrons who wished to dine in. Near the entrance was the usual counter where customers would queue up for takeaway food – mostly a piece of fish and a bag of chips fried in oil, which suited the palates of its discerning clientele, as well as bowls of mouth-watering home-made pickled cucumbers. Outside, there was a large forecourt where youngsters used to congregate and where many love affairs were started, developed and in some cases dramatically terminated. After snacking on a bag of chips Leslie would walk Anita home.

Leslie opened the letter with anticipation not recognising the handwriting, and gave a cry of delight at seeing Anita's name. She wrote, "Now the war in Europe has finished and there is evidence that the conflict in the Far East will soon be coming to an end, I would like to know what your intentions are." It gradually crossed his mind that Anita was putting her cards firmly on the table and he was impressed, intrigued and amused.

"If you want to marry me then I will be happy to marry you", she continued, "but if marriage isn't your objective, you mustn't worry because there is another boy in Leeds, who has just returned from the Atlantic, who has made clear his desire to marry me."

One aspect that impressed Leslie was that Anita took the initiative and wasn't coy about standing up for herself. She had a feisty side to her character and he admired that, but most of all she was not thinking merely about the here and now but planning how to move her own life forward. It was a very tempting offer and Leslie had no hesitation in agreeing to the proposition, mainly because he had been fighting for four years and he also needed to move on with his life. He had been in some dangerous situations and had made a few life-threatening decisions, and he felt he was now his own man. Many other servicemen held the same opinion – they went into the forces as boys and came out as men. Those who wanted to return to previous jobs were few and far between. The world was a dark, grey place; rationing had been brought in but one thing remained constant – almost everyone was optimistic about the future.

There had also been a tremendous political change in the country with the shock victory for Labour in the 1945 general election The outcome of the election proved to be a political bombshell. Only twelve weeks earlier Winston Churchill had announced the unconditional surrender of Nazi Germany. He wanted his wartime coalition to continue until Japan also had been defeated but was not unduly dismayed when Labour ministers insisted that the country be offered a democratic option. The Prime Minister called the election for early July confident that the electorate would back him, the greatest hero of the hour. The result was definitely not Churchill's finest hour.

Engagement of Anita
Feddy and Leslie, 1946

After all he had endured, the prospect of returning home to live with his parents seemed alien. Furthermore, there was another important factor to consider – Leslie realised that he was very much in love with Anita. He told his mother of his intention and said that he would use his RAF pay cheque to buy Anita an engagement ring.

Consequently, on 31 August 1946, a year prior to his demobilisation, Leslie married his long-time sweetheart Anita in the Chassidishe Synagogue in Spencer Place, Chapeltown, Leeds.

Uncle Ashy and his wife Sarah were among the wedding guests. Ashy, travelling from Manchester to be at the wedding, was still considered to be the family rebel after breaking away from the family in the East End to go and work in Lancashire.

Ashy was again to shock the family, particularly Harry. Taking him quietly aside at the reception, he announced that his wife Sarah was pregnant. Harry, spluttering over his cherry brandy, was horrified. There was Leslie, his bridegroom son of twenty-one, and here was Ashy, Harry's eldest brother who was in his late forties, telling him that his wife was with child. That wasn't the 'done thing', he thought, what was the world coming to?

Other guests at the wedding were Bessie's sister and her husband, Joe Kutner. After posing for a family photograph and picking up a whisky-sour, Uncle Joe asked Leslie what his plans were after he was finally demobbed in 1947.

Wedding of Leslie and Anita at Spencer Place
Synagogue, 31 August 1946

"I don't know, Uncle Joe, but one thing is certain, I'm not going back into the clothing trade. I'll get a job as a salesman somewhere, I suppose."

Joe worked as a production and development chemist for a small nitro-cellulose company in the East End called Nuagane Products, which made nitro-cellulose leather coatings and cellulose lacquers. "Why don't you come into the paint trade?" he suggested. Leslie was taken aback: "The paint trade? I'm not too sure about that – for one thing, I don't know anything at all about the paint industry."

Joe told him to put aside his uncertainty – this was the chance for him to learn. "You can set up a little warehouse somewhere in Leeds and my company will supply you with cellulose thinners which you can then sell." The proposed deal was that, as wholesalers, Nuagane Products would supply Leslie, who in turn would sell the thinners at a nice profit. He told him there was a national shortage for the car refinishing market and added: "I know you will do well." The shortage, Joe continued, would give Leslie an easy market and he forecast that in three years' time he would be able to retire.

This gave Leslie food for thought and he sat down later and considered the pros and cons. It was certainly a challenge, he thought, and one clear motivating factor was that if he took up the offer then he could get his foot on the bottom rung of the ladder and climb to the top, no matter how hard the ascent. The break of going into the Services and seeing the world at large, as well as having the opportunity of travelling and meeting people from different walks of life, had given him a new perspective, making him realise more than ever that there was more to life if he was willing to work hard for it. His uncle had offered him the prospect of enjoying a comfortable living, as well as giving him hope for his family's future. The possibility of economic success beyond anything that his parents and grandparents had ever achieved now filled him with expectation.

That was all the incentive Leslie needed, because to him money was simply a fortuitous by-product of success. All he asked was to make a decent living. Needless to say, in the years that followed, Leslie went on to make rather a lot of money, but job satisfaction was always the key issue and, in the scheme of things, the most important element in his combination of vision and endurance.

Three

Developing Business & Family

THE YEAR 1947 BROUGHT THE worst snowfall ever seen in the 20th century in the United Kingdom with extensive travel disruption. The wintry conditions were never-ending, lasting until mid-March, and although many snow scenes looked very nice on picture postcards, in reality it became something that people were happy to consign to the history books.

In February, Leslie was demobilised with a gratuity of £250. The day after he regained his freedom, he combined this hand-out with the money put aside from his RAF whisky enterprise and, with support from family members as well as from Uncle Joe who chipped in another £250, the available capital amounted to £1,000. Using this money to get started in business, Leslie formed the Silver Paint and Lacquer Company Ltd.

After he obtained the raw materials, Leslie set about renting an old stable from Craven Dairies in upper North Street off Woodhouse Lane. He realised that Silver Paint and Lacquer Company Ltd was 'a stupid name' but he was given no choice in the matter, because when he came to register the company he had to submit ten potential names as there were so many companies being formed; all of them had Silver and Paint in the title and the name he hurriedly picked hadn't been selected by any other business. However, he thought, what's in a name; building up the business was his main concern. So Leslie, who had previously never sold anything other than books, focussed on buying and selling – he bought the paint thinners at twelve shillings a gallon and sold them at fifteen shillings. Nuagane shipped up supplies of thinners and Leslie sold them on. This then was to become Leslie's way of life.

Leslie and Anita went to live in a first-floor flat at 24 Reginald Terrace in Chapeltown. Anita was happy to become involved in the business and used her secretarial skills to type out invoices. Things were rolling merrily along for Leslie as his young wife continued to be a wonderful asset in the day-to-day running of the business and gave him tremendous support. Vivacious and convivial, she would often accompany him to business meetings. These went beyond the usual 'meet and greet' convention and often involved entertaining clients at luncheons and dinners.

However, there was a disappointment on the way when a year after starting the enterprise Leslie received a business-changing phone call. It was from Uncle Joe saying he could not supply him anymore because of the logistics of providing cellulose thinners at wholesale prices. One of Nuagane's directors, Allan Brent, had argued that with the shortage of raw materials, why ship to Leeds when his firm could sell all they could produce in the London area, and get themselves a full price and save on transport too.

Joe suggested that Leslie went into the manufacturing of thinners, an idea which Leslie at first rejected for the simple reason that he didn't know how to go about it. "Leslie, listen to me, as an ex-serviceman you will receive an allocation of raw materials and all you need is the formula. You get a ninety-gallon barrel and a semi-rotary pump, to which you add different chemicals and pump them into the barrel. You then agitate the solvents, blend them well and then you pour the mixture out into cans." The cost of manufacturing would be eight shillings a gallon, plus a shilling for the can, and Leslie could sell retail at up to one pound a gallon. "It's simplicity itself", said Uncle Joe.

Leslie was not in a position to shilly-shally – he had to give it a go. A thirty-by-thirty foot stable could not last forever and, as the first part-time employees were recruited it became crowded enough to prompt one of many relocations. Leslie had come across a dilapidated building belonging to the Leeds Fireclay Company in Burmantofts in Leeds and rented a part of the building. Some months later, Uncle Joe gave Leslie a further challenge. He had invested £250 in the business and told Leslie that with his brother Stanley's demob on the horizon,

Leslie and Harry with the SPL van, 1950

he assumed that his younger brother would be joining the business. Perhaps this would be a good time for Joe to sell his share. He was quite happy to receive back his original investment. Harry, always the honourable gentleman, insisted that Leslie give him a fair return for his twelve-month investment and a sum of £325 was handed over. Leslie always joked that if Uncle Joe, who was more than delighted to receive such a handsome return, had realised that in sixty years time his £250 investment would have been worth millions, he might not have been quite so elated. Some you win, some you lose!

There were many other paint companies operating in Leeds during this period, but they weren't specialising in the type of work in which SPL was engaged. Consequently, after mixing the magic solvents in the morning, Leslie would transform his casual image and become a sharp-suited, savvy salesman painting the town silver in his search for new customers.

His market was the second-hand car business and he called into garages like Appleyards on Regent Street that used cellulose thinners for re-painting vehicles. Leslie discovered that his customers were also interested in car re-finishes. Having sought advice, he bought twin whirlpool mixers from an engineering company called Sydney Smith with a view to making clear lacquers. He then purchased other machines for pigment dispersion from Binny Smith and Ashby and bought in paralac resins from ICI. The world was indeed his oyster but some twelve-months later the boom in the second-hand car market collapsed. Suddenly, he and his business associates realised that they had very few customers left. However, Leslie had noticed that Leeds had a highly thriving furniture industry which led him into researching cellulose furniture lacquers. This prompted a slow and steady recovery.

With the purchase of new machinery and modern technology, the product range developed and decorative paint manufacturing commenced. Towards the end of the 1950s, the business recognised that the paint industry was evolving. Gradually, Leslie and the company drifted into decorative products. Emulsions were replacing distemper, and by this time the company's equipment had increased. This included acquiring a couple of small ball-mills for making primers and, from Vickers, a single-roll grinding machine.

Leslie was approached by a small supermarket owner on New York Road called Barry Baker. He was looking for cheap paint to put on his shelves, along with other DIY products, and wondered if Leslie could help. Feeling less than confident, Leslie decided to give it a whirl, producing a range of six colours in emulsion and gloss and three colours in undercoat. Unsure whether the products would sell on price alone in competition with the big-boy brand leaders of the day, he nevertheless had a low-cost label printed. Within forty-eight hours, not only did Baker repeat the order but, to Leslie's amazement, he trebled it. Suddenly, his paint became desirable. The success of the products, selling at some 30% below the brand leaders' prices, motivated Leslie to produce an attractively decorated tin. Low-cost emulsion, which Leslie proudly claimed as 'our innovation' opened up a new market, as did an export trade with West Africa which was soon followed by North Africa, the Gulf and the Middle-East.

The opportunity for entry into the decorative paint market was helped enormously by the Resale Price Maintenance (RPM) Act which had recently come into force. RPM is a practice whereby a manufacturer and its distributors agree that the latter will sell the manufacturer's product at certain prices, at or above a minimum resale price maintenance. If a reseller refuses to maintain prices, either openly or covertly, the manufacturer may cease doing business with the firm. The cream of the crop brand leaders – Dulux, Bergers, Magicote and Crown – were all being sold retail at fixed prices, pre-set by the manufacturers.

Meanwhile, something else was happening in the continually changing retail world. The presence of UK supermarkets was widening as their businesses cultivated discounting on food. Once they looked beyond food, paint proved to be an obvious target. As different paint manufacturers sold their products through an established chain – from manufacturers to a regional wholesaler and then on to a recognised retailer, all at fixed prices – this was a setup that left the door wide open for the non-branded market and the introduction of those magical words 'cut-price'.

By now Leslie was fizzing with energy and thought of the name Home Charm by chance when, after Baker's introduction, he started selling competitively to other supermarkets. But he needed a name to go on the tin, and after one or two buyers described the product as 'charming', Leslie thought that Home Charm would serve that purpose. However he soon found himself attacked from all quarters; what he didn't realise was that he was playing with dynamite. The Grocer magazine displayed the wave of disapproval by running a front-page article sarcastically headlined "A Packet of Marg and a Pint of Home Charm, Please." The firm was also widely criticised within the industry, but the proof of the paint was in the painting – sales increased and Leslie was to experience a period of great commercial success.

All of this success necessitated looking around for new premises as the company had outgrown its drying-shed factory in Leeds. There were new products to develop and sell. Leslie and his team were striking out and investing in the future and this included moving the company to Batley and new premises. The Batley plant, purchased for about £3,000, was about twelve miles from the original site and had been a converted former shoddy-mill. Batley had depended on shoddy, a process whereby cloth was made out of recycled rags for well over 100 years, but this had suffered a sad collapse and most of the old mills were neglected and deserted due to the invasion of modern technology. On one cold wet weekend in 1961 the plant was moved from Leeds and the business continued to thrive by selling decorative products through supermarket outlets.

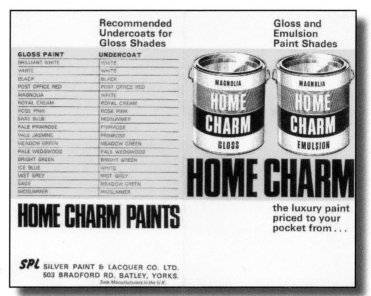

An early 1960's Home Charm colour chart

The previous year (1960), sales revenue had reached the £100,000 mark for the first time and the future looked rosy. Leslie had been in business for thirteen years which he termed 'a long hard apprenticeship'. A small technical staff had already been engaged and remained very loyal, continually delivering an excellent product at a price that could be sold competitively – this was to be SPL's forte.

What happened next would change the company's direction internationally. One of Leslie's customers from the mining industry in Doncaster introduced him to a small company in Nigeria. The firm was initially interested in importing cellulose thinners and through an exchange of correspondence and phone calls a satisfactory deal was struck. Leslie's bank was very helpful in instructing him on what to look out for and how to handle the documentation. The initial orders went through reasonably well and after a couple of transactions it was felt that possibly a personal visit from Leslie would be an added advantage. It was also pointed out that not much would be attached to the airfare costs if Leslie visited other countries en route – it was a bold idea and consequently an extended 'grand tour' was organised. The trip, in 1963-64, took over a month and included flying out to Port Harcourt in Nigeria and returning via Lagos, Accra in Ghana, Sierra Leona, Libya and Malta. But things did not run smoothly. Some issues were domestic, such as the need to obtain contacts from

Export packing of
Home Charm paints

the Department of Trade and other sources. But the real concern was
that by the time Leslie had returned home, and much to everyone's
surprise, no orders had been booked. Management blamed its
inexperience in selling to other countries. Nevertheless, following
his despondent return, Leslie decided to give his contacts a little push
and within a few days the orders started trickling in. There were sighs
of relief all round and Leslie brought out the whisky bottle and he
and his team had a drink to celebrate.

By this time, Anita's involvement in the business was proving
indispensible. With her quiet demeanour and cool charm she had by
now become a considerable asset and continued to accompany Leslie
when there were clients to be wined and dined. Anita's history of
rheumatic fever had left her with troublesome leaking heart valves.
She suffered bouts of extreme exhaustion which were worrying, but
she miraculously managed to conceal this when out with clients. On
these occasions she had such an intense adrenalin rush that by the
time they returned home she would quite often be so worn out that
it was left to Leslie to undress her and put her to bed.

～ ～ ～

Business continued to make satisfactory progress and financial
figures were looking robust. It had taken thirteen years to achieve
the first £100,000 but during the next fourteen years they went from
£100,000 to a leap of £7 million - a very healthy rate of growth. By

1967 the firm's revenues had reached well over £400,000 and there was further good news to come because in 1970 revenues had topped the million mark. SPL had developed a broad knowledge of how to produce a range of industrial and decorative products which were not only attractive to the domestic market but which were also found to be readily acceptable overseas. By this time the original nitro-cellulose business had become just a minor part of the enterprise and decorative products had become the firm's bread and butter.

Although they had moved into new premises in Batley in 1961, it only took five years for Leslie to realise that, once again, he had a problem with space. This was caused by the development of the decorative product range and an increasing export market, particularly in low-cost emulsions. Leslie's dictum was always to move with the times, so it was fortuitous that next to the existing building was a 100,000 square foot factory together with a main road office block which Leslie liked very much and which after close inspection he managed to acquire freehold for a mere £10,000. Needless to say it was a bargain.

For the first time he had an efficient four-storey plant designed on a flow system where raw materials were hoisted to the floor on which they were to be used, finishing with ground-floor filling-lines leading into a ground-floor warehouse with despatch amenities. Now in possession of main road access, a modern office and a superb laboratory block. Leslie and his team thought that all of their dreams had come true. A few months after SPL were up and running in the new factory a further 100,000 square foot mill behind the factory became available and Leslie thought that it would make an ideal tin and raw materials store. This was available at a price of £17,000 and Leslie, with his thoughts on investing in the future, immediately snapped it up.

By sheer chance Leslie had met a Leeds United fan, Alan Greenside, who happened to be the buying director for Block & Quayle, which was a do-it-yourself and home improvement retailing company which was just opening its first outlet in Portswood, Southampton. The firm, founded by Richard Block and David Quayle in 1969, soon shortened its name to B&Q and Leslie did a deal with them. Providing they didn't undersell SPL's prices he would give them a significant discount. Both parties adhered to their promises, which were based

Warehouse at 513 Bradford Road, with Home Charm tins in background

on trust, and B&Q became one of the firm's largest and most loyal customers for many years.

During the late sixties and early seventies things had continued to go well for SPL. Whereas traditional markets for cellulose products remained at best stable, the decorative products division was flying high on the back of the huge UK market. This was also the start of the property boom and people were buying, building and developing like there was no tomorrow – and the icing on the cake, of course, was that all these properties needed maintaining and that involved many coats of paint. Furthermore, the highly competitive range of export products, helped enormously by a weak pound, was growing fast.

All of this meant that there was a large consumption of polymers, the raw material for emulsion paint. Fundamentally, a polymer is a large molecule composed of many sub-units known as monomers. Polymers range from familiar synthetic plastics such as polystyrene (used in Styrofoam) to natural biopolymers such as shellac, amber and cellulose. In the UK there were three main suppliers of polymers and Leslie soon discovered that SPL had become the largest customer for the firm BP Polymers. To enhance its credibility, SPL persuaded BP to allow SPL to use their brand motif on its packaging, and this greatly improved supermarket sales. But unknown to SPL, BP

Polymers was actually losing money on polymers and had decided to sell the business to its main competitor, Vinyl Products.

The next thing Leslie knew was that one morning in the early 1970s he received a very friendly visit from a Mr Ford, managing director of Vinyl. After observing the niceties, a long chat ensued about the sale of the business, during which it was stated that Vinyl wanted to continue with SPL's business. In return, Leslie expressed the hope that both companies would get on well together, trusting that the previous contract with BP would continue to be honoured. But Mr Ford's reply came as something of a bombshell. Putting his cards on the table, he warned that the price would regrettably have to be increased to a level that was roughly 20% above what was currently being charged.

So far as Leslie was concerned there were no such things as problems, only solutions. After taking on board this unwelcome news, his instinctive reaction was to think: "If only we could make our own polymer then our financial problem would disappear." So although they parted amicably, Leslie was already deep in thought. After a few minutes he called in the technical staff which comprised Eric Smith, SPL's technical director, Gordon Bentley the production director and Cecil (Ces) Butler who was the firm's industrial coatings chemist. Leslie sat behind his desk and, looking directly at them, asked: "What do you have to do to make polymers?" to which Ces quickly replied that the firm was far too small even to consider it. Gordon, who had joined the firm in 1960 as a works manager, was forever the pessimist. His past remark that "making low cost emulsions would bankrupt the firm" was still lodged in Leslie's mind. True to form, Gordon warned that "it was the quick route into liquidation." However, Eric, a first class chemist who had joined the company direct from school, said that while he wasn't sure about what was involved he would like to find out more about the proposition and promised to investigate and report back. Sure enough, two days later, Eric came into Leslie's office and declared: "Leslie, I've looked into the polymer-emulsion technicalities and it really doesn't look all that complicated." He smiled, leant forward and confided: "In fact, I've got one of the lads in the lab working on it right now."

It only took a few days for Eric to return with a test-tube containing a milky substance which he held up proudly and said: "Leslie, you are looking at our first batch of polymers." This was to be the development which led the business on to even greater growth.

BUILDING A FAMILY

Anita had always been advised by her family doctor not to have any children because she had a heart condition which was the consequence of contracting rheumatic fever as a child and which had caused permanent damage. Consequently, it became a bit of a dilemma when, in late 1947, she fell pregnant with Hilary.

Instead of bed-rest, Anita insisted on continuing working, which as a young pregnant mum presented numerous problems like making frequent trips to the privy. At that time, the Torre Road factory was situated up a steep slope, which iced up very badly in the winter. The men at the factory were well provided for with toilet facilities; however, the women fared less well. The nearest lavatories were situated in the cinema and corner shop which were located down the slope and along the road. Anita, having to continually don winter clothing to go and spend the proverbial penny, always joked she was 'inconvenienced' when navigating the slippery slope.

She and Leslie were residing in Reginald Terrace when Hilary was born on 29 June 1948, the year the state of Israel was formed. Anita's insistence on working in the company had been frowned upon, particularly by her medical advisors, and she had been put on a strict regime of resting and taking care herself during the latter part of the pregnancy. Her return to robust health was a bit of a worry and quite a slow procedure after Hilary came into the world.

As a child, Hilary was more aware of her parents' social and Zionist inclinations than those pertaining to religion. Nevertheless, the family retained a strong Jewish identity and worshipped on high holy days at a synagogue in Spencer Place in Chapeltown, where Anita's family were stalwart members. Because of Leslie and Anita's association with Poale Zion, the forerunner of the Jewish Labour Movement, Hilary became a member of Young Poale Zion.

Her weekends also involved supporting Leeds United and in her early teens she was given a special 'eldest-child treat' of visiting Elland Road with Leslie. But first the two-some had to make a stop at the sweet shop prior to sitting with other spectators to share in the excitement, thrill or despair of the matches. At these thrilling outings, Hilary's love of football and Leeds United were forged. It was to become a passion she shared with her father that has lasted a lifetime.

Hilary attended a local primary school and was showered with great love and pride after being the first grandchild in the family to pass her 11-plus examination, prior to attending Allerton High School which led on to further education. She always appreciated the support and advice her father gave to her in whichever direction she chose to take her schooling. In spite of later becoming a Chancellor of the Leeds Metropolitan University, Leslie had always been in awe of further education. However, he maintained that if he had become a teacher, which is something he once hankered after, he would have missed the enormous pleasure he enjoyed as a paint manufacturer.

After leaving school Hilary went to Bradford College of Art which led to attending Birmingham College of Art to study textile design. It was there she met Oded Brosh, an Israeli student studying business studies. They married in 1970 and moved to London where Hilary continued her studies and where their first daughter, Talya, was born in 1973. In 1977 they returned to Leeds and Oded started working for SPL in the purchasing department. Their second daughter Karen was born in 1977 and a third daughter Lisa was born in 1979. Hilary and Oded eventually divorced and in 2004 Hilary married Peter Curwen.

Anita's second pregnancy, with Jane, came a bit sooner than expected. When she discovered she was pregnant again, Anita became quite perturbed. Not only did she have to negotiate the pram down or up one flight of stairs each time she left or returned home, but she wasn't sure how her health would cope in the future months. Doctors continually disapproved and wagged a constant 'who's a naughty girl' finger at her.

Turning to her mother for advice, Anita walked to Trafford Terrace in Harehills, where her parents lived, to lament her condition. Her mother Millie sat her down, made a strong cuppa, listened to her daughter's concerns, nodded her head in sympathy and then, to Anita's dismay, sent her back home with a stark rebuke. Instead of the customary tea and sympathy she was longing to receive, Anita came away with a strong lecture about marital duties, taking the rough with the smooth and something about 'you've made your bed, now lie in it' thrown in for good measure. She was warned not to have any more children, indeed quite frankly she was cautioned not to marry at all, and now she must accept the consequences.

In spite of her doctors' reservations, Anita was proceeding reasonably satisfactorily towards her second childbirth. However, she had accepted the need to take lots of bed-rest during her confinement with her disapproving mother, Millie, becoming a regular visitor, giving what help she could. Jane was born on 25 January 1950 and family members were overjoyed.

Fortuitously, just before Jane was born, the opportunity to move into the Moortown area arose when Leslie and Anita were offered a house at 19s 2d rent a week on the Deanswood council estate, which they accepted with gratitude. The house, in Deanswood Place on the corner of a cul-de-sac, had an ample garden in which proud Leslie showed off his green fingers with a magnificent display of home-grown vegetables and fruit, particularly rhubarb. Although now working long, arduous hours at SPL, he managed to become active in the residents' association on the estate, and he helped organise many expeditions such as weekend outings with neighbours and friends to Ilkley Moor and the Yorkshire countryside.

Jane enjoyed a happy childhood and, after leaving Allerton Grange School, she attended the North of England Secretarial College where she was given a commercial education. In due course, she was interviewed for a job as a secretary to a large company but, unfortunately, the company went bust the day before Jane was supposed to start work. At that time, Leslie was paying a temporary worker to do his secretarial work so he suggested to Jane that she start

Leslie, Anita and Jane at home in 9 Deanswood Place

Leslie, Hilary and Jane in the
garden at 9 Deanswood Place

temping for him instead. Jane thought the idea was attractive and
said she'd 'give it a go'. She stayed with the company until she married
in 1973. Starting out as her father's secretary, she then moved on as
assistant to Lyn Beaumont in the export department. Jane launched
the Personnel Department – a world full of staff records and wages,
all done by hand, calculators and tax tables, and putting cash into
envelopes each week. It was quite daunting to get the right amount
of notes and coins to make up the wages, and a veteran office worker
used to catch Jane out quite often, saying she was one penny out
with his wages. Jane thought he went to sleep reading the HMRC
tax tables.

Another task was to arrange the company functions which
included Christmas dances, anniversary parties and so forth,
sometimes for over 200 guests at Selby Fork, a favourite location.
She and Leslie made an ideal meet-and-greet couple. Jane used to
stand behind Leslie at the door and with clip-board in hand provided
the names of the people who were coming in. A particular expertise
was matching up each couple correctly. She was on the ball most of
the time, but became used to getting a black look from Leslie if she
mis-matched a couple erroneously.

Until she passed her driving test, Jane and Leslie used to go into
work together. Leslie was eventually persuaded to let her drive in on
L-plates. Jane and her dad struck up a deal about the car radio though.
Leslie had Radio Two on until the pair got to the other side of Leeds,

and then it was the great changeover and Jane was allowed to tune into Radio One. Not surprisingly, Leslie was relieved when Jane passed her driving test the first time round, and she was allowed to drive Anita's Triumph Spitfire.

Jane met Donald Komrower prior to his taking his finals. Donald then went off to do VSO in Uganda and Jane went to visit him for a month, returning in January 1972. Donald returned from Africa in January 1973 for Mark's Bar Mitzvah celebrations and it was for this occasion that Jane gave him an ultimatum; if he didn't return to be her escort at the thirteenth-birthday ceremony then she suggested they call it quits. That was a warning Donald couldn't ignore and the couple became engaged in February 1973 and married in July. They relocated to Derby where Donald worked for British Celanese while Jane found employment with Raleigh Industries. A couple of years later Leslie asked Donald to help him start up the polymer side of the business and he came on board proving to be a great asset.

Leslie and Anita got on well with Jane's in-laws, Diana and Arthur Komrower and to celebrate the Labour victory in the October 1974 general election the Komrower's invited Leslie and Anita to dinner at their home. Jane and Donald were already there waiting and standing at the window they suddenly saw the flash of a car's headlights. It was Leslie pulling into the driveway in his first ever Rolls Royce. There were cheers and laughter as the quartet noticed the added touch of a red rosette sticking proudly on the car bonnet. The Rolls had been bought prior to Jane's marriage and it cost just a few hundred pounds more than her first house in Derby – the house cost £9,299 and the Rolls slightly more at £9,500.

With the business thriving, the family decided, in 1959, to move from Deanswood Place to the more up-market location of Sandhill Oval in Alwoodley. The accommodation offered the luxury of more rooms and extra space.

On 26 February 1960, ten years after having Jane, Anita gave birth to Mark in their new home. It was the custom at that period for women to have their babies when they were in their twenties, but not uncommon that those in their late thirties found themselves pregnant. Once again Anita's pregnancy gave concern. She was severely warned to take to her bed and rest as much as possible and was put under constant medical supervision.

The family were delighted to welcome a boy at last. As one would have expected, the new addition to the family grew up surrounded by the love of doting parents, a resident grandfather – Anita's mother Millie had died just before Mark was born and Anita had brought her father Fred to live permanently in the new house – and two affectionate sisters, some ten or more years his senior. Mark was a much treasured little boy with both his sisters and his grandfather at his constant beck and call. It was the 'little mothers' who took over parental control when Leslie and Anita had to be absent from home – business commitments and the demand of running an export business meant that Leslie and Anita were frequently away overseas.

As she was looked upon as an older mother, Anita was to confide to Leslie a few years later that, when doing the school-run with Mark, she felt 'more like a grandmother than a mother.' Leslie, on the other hand, was in his element. After a decade in a household that was dominated by the distaff side, he at last had the pleasure of his young son's company to kick a football to his heart's content in the privacy of his own back yard.

Mark was educated at Giggleswick School, later moving to INSEAD Business School near Paris. He started working in the family business in January 1977 and Leslie insisted that he start on the bottom rung of the ladder, so his initial job was filling white spirit bottles. When Mark decided to leave the business in 1990, his final job was running the chemicals division with 180 employees.

His first marriage took place in 1983 and lasted for roughly seven years, producing two children, Hannah and Alex. His second marriage was to Tina in 1991, and the couple had three children – Rosie, Maisie and Ben. Two years later, Mark created the Academy Health Club which was, and remains, a large private health club and spa in nearby Harrogate. In 1999, he acquired and developed the five-star Hotel Le Mas Candille in Vieux Mougins, near Cannes, which opened in 2002. At this point he and his family moved to France to live in the vicinity of the hotel. He also used his business acumen to be involved in various real estate businesses.

～ ～ ～

Leslie and Anita passed down great values to their children, but the sense of family and the importance of cementing family ties were foremost. They also showed them, by example, the importance of being valuable community members and certainly not afraid of getting involved in community matters and standing up to social injustice. For example, they were really supportive of Jane's efforts with the Jewish Youth Voluntary Service and always welcomed her friends into the house with warmth, interest, respect and many genuine enquiries about the work in which she and the organisation was involved in.

Anita was wonderful with her children even though she wasn't well enough to do as much as she wanted. And although Leslie was always proud of his children's achievements, at whatever level, Anita quite

Family group in Sandmoor Avenue, 1978.
Standing- Donald Komrower, Leslie, Oded Brosh,
sitting- Mark, Jane, Anita, Hilary, in front: Jenny, Adam, Karen and Talya

often used him as a threat. If something happened that displeased her, she would say to them: "Just you wait till dad gets home." It was meant as a warning but somehow it never really troubled the three siblings because they knew their dad would be sympathetic.

By this time Leslie thought himself more of a Yorkshireman than an East Ender; in fact, his one regret was that he hadn't been born in Leeds, so ingrained was the city in his DNA.

Four

Business Expansion

LESLIE'S RELATIONSHIPS WITH HIS STAFF were always cordial, and he takes great pride in the fact that his employees never went on strike. One of his most important employees was arguably Eric Smith who first met Leslie in 1958 when he joined Silver Paint and Lacquer. At that time the company was primarily involved in the manufacture of industrial and automotive paints. Eric worked with Leslie right up to the time he retired and was able to see at first-hand the remarkable progress made in developing and expanding the start-up company during his 33-year tenure.

In the early 1960s, the paint industry was very seasonal but Leslie went on to pioneer the idea of developing overseas markets, mostly in Africa and the Middle East, to maintain production levels and profitability through the winter months. Eric always thought that the fact that SPL was able to grow so successfully and to invest in, and pioneer, new and industry-leading approaches to paint manufacture was undoubtedly due to Leslie's personal qualities and his ability to choose the right people and create teams that would work well together. Importantly, the company's success was also to bring employment and prosperity to the towns of Morley, Batley and Birstall.

Through his own hard work and 'can-do' attitude Leslie, who was making use of SPL's financial scope to invest in the future, had been an inspiration to all those who came in contact with him, be they employees, customers or competitors. His relaxed and fair style of management engendered respect from employees at all levels. It was

Eric Smith as a young chemist at SPL

very much a sofa government, very informal, very laid-back, but nevertheless stringently organised as well.

Gladys Hall was a cleaner, who was not only employed to give the offices and staff room a 'good once over', but also happened, in 1967-68, to be married to the Mayor of Batley, Harold Hall. At that time, the Mayor received no remuneration for the honour of being appointed the town's first citizen and accordingly had to hold down normal, everyday jobs and fit these into the mayoral schedule as best they could. Instead of vacating his office until Gladys had completed her chores, Leslie would often hang around and engage her in conversation. The talk, of course, was political but Leslie was also interested in hearing her family and civic news and would often joke about the Mayoress cleaning his office.

Gladys, in turn, would discuss mayoral news especially her husband's plans, unveiled in his first speech to Batley Town Council in May 1967, about the redevelopment of Batley and Birstall town centres, the addition of off-street parking and the improvement of car parks. There were plans in the pipeline for adding park areas in Henrietta Street, Wilton Street and Low Lane in Birstall of which Leslie heartily approved. If it was for the greater good of the community, Leslie was all for it.

He continued to take a genuine interest in the couple's many civic engagements such as opening the new Trustee Savings Bank and Batley Carr library as well as officiating at many prize presentations to scouts, beauty queens and bowling clubs, in addition to switching on Batley's Christmas lights.

To Gladys, Leslie was just 'the boss' who never put himself on a pedestal. There was certainly no class divide and Gladys respected this; to her he wasn't just an employer and friend, he was 'a man of the people'.

Harold Teale was a driver employed at SPL at Batley. When he was diagnosed with stomach cancer, he continued to work until things got too bad and he became housebound. Not up to receiving many visitors, Harold said to his daughter Julie that the only person he wanted to see was his boss and friend 'Mr Leslie'. So without an appointment, Julie went to see Leslie. She explained to the receptionist the reason for her visit, who in turn reported to Leslie the severity of Harold's illness. Leslie immediately ordered his chauffer to bring his car round to the front entrance and, with Julie and her daughter comfortably seated in the back of the car, drove to Harold's home. Leslie stayed for about an hour talking to Harold, taking a genuine interest in the details of his illness, and on his return to the office summoned the rest of his drivers and told them of Harold's disease. The next day, all the drivers gathered together and made a concerted effort to visit Harold just days before his death. Leslie's remarkable interest in all his employees was to make a deep impression on them for the decades that followed.

Alex Mowat had one over-riding memory of Leslie when he was a junior programmer at Kalon in 1989. Bumping into Leslie in a corridor the day after Alex's first son was born, Leslie asked him what he was looking so pleased about. Alex explained that he had become a new dad, upon which Leslie congratulated him. A couple of years later, Leslie was to see Alex again and was told that his wife had given birth to their second son. Leslie offered his congratulations and remarked: "Let me see, your elder son must be two years old now." Alex was staggered to hear how his boss had remembered something that was of no direct relevance to him. The incident made a huge impression on Alex and was something he never forgot.

John Robinson was also impressed by Leslie's fine communication skills. He joined the company in 1971, initially as a sales representative with Leslie's newly formed chemical division, Smyth Morris Chemicals, which shared the offices and facilities of SPL at their Burrows Mill site on Bradford Road, Batley. John was quickly introduced to the ethos of the company when Leslie told him: "Look here John, you will enjoy yourself working for me and I'm sure you'll do very well. But always remember that for every pound you generate there are twenty shillings – you can have one of those shillings but I want the other nineteen." As John rose through the ranks to become sales director of Smyth Morris Chemicals, his contact with Leslie increased and reinforced his opinion that Leslie was determined to become one of the leading players within the paint industry.

Leslie was nothing if not generous to all his employees and many of the younger members arrived at church on their wedding day in Leslie's gleaming Rolls Royce with chauffeur Malcolm at the wheel.

For the sales team there were annual trips to Majorca, complete with spouses and partners, to attend the company's annual sales conferences during an unforgettable weekend in the sun. Leslie would address the conference, usually with the theme 'Work hard – play hard.' And this they certainly did. Indeed, in those early days, most employees were eager to put in a Saturday morning shift in order to help develop the business.

While being extremely generous Leslie could also be very careful. John recalls the time that Bessie Sheldon, the Mayor of Batley, requested a factory tour. Instead of a slap-up do and a glass of champagne afterwards, Leslie arranged to take Bessie on a visit to the next door pub, The Victoria, for a drink where the real ale flowed.

When, in the 1980s the firm moved to the Birstall site, the new premises provided a touch of luxury after all the years on Bradford Road, since it included modern offices, a new plant and parking for all. Leslie still retained his original values and toured the offices and works most days, stopping to chat as he did his rounds. By this time he had been installed as Leeds United Chairman and would pop into John's office to discuss the latest transfer news at Elland Road even though John was a Bradford City supporter. Leslie engaged very closely with the local community, hosting many Christmas parties in the canteen at Birstall for staff and some

Billie, a long term employee in the Bradford Road factory

neighbours in the vicinity of the new site, where they would enjoy a sumptuous Christmas dinner served by the directors.

In 1982, the Group said goodbye to Ces Butler, who retired as SPL personnel director after thirteen years with the company. Ces was a highly popular member of staff and to mark the occasion a special dinner was held at Walton Hall Country Club for Ces, his wife Louise and his family and friends. The event was attended by over sixty SPL directors, colleagues and their wives. Ces got his retirement off to a breezy start when Leslie presented him with tickets for a luxury cruise for two.

It is worth noting the attitude of his employees to the trappings of wealth that Leslie acquired, such as his Rolls Royce and chauffeur. Far from expressing envy, employees were much gratified that their boss looked like the successful businessman that he was. Their view was that they wanted outsiders to understand that they worked for a thriving business, and were well paid for doing so. They absolutely did not want 'the boss' to drive around in a Ford Escort.

BUSINESS IN THE 1970S

The 1970s were desperately difficult years for Britain, both economically and politically. After losing the 1970 general election to Edward Heath, Harold Wilson had spent four years as leader of the opposition. Edward Heath came to power promising a 'quiet revolution' that would turn around the fortunes of the country. However Sailor Ted soon ran aground, his ship scuppered by the lethal combination of an energy crisis, a financial crash and a second miners' strike in two years. The general election of February 1974 resulted in a hung parliament with Wilson returning to power as leader of a minority government and a second general election followed in the autumn which resulted in a narrow Labour victory.

By that time, SPL was using over 2,500 tonnes of polymers a year. Having made the decision to start manufacturing polymers from then on it was all systems go. SPL acquired further premises in Batley and, with a budget of around £200,000, started building a small polymer plant with two reactors and sufficient storage capacity. But there was bad news on the horizon. They were halfway through the construction when a chemical plant close to the village of Flixborough, Lincolnshire blew up. The explosion on 1 June 1974 killed twenty-eight people and thirty-six were seriously injured. The plant, in operation since 1967, produced caprolactam, a precursor chemical used in the manufacturer of nylon. Village residents had never been happy to have such a large industrial development so close to their homes and had expressed grave concern when the plant was first proposed. At last, they felt they had been vindicated but, nonetheless, despite many protests, mostly at top-level, the plant was rebuilt, only to close a few years later. The devastating explosion resulted in the government hastily introducing new safety rules for chemical plants which served, effectively, to double SPL's costs. Consequently, there was relentless financial pressure and the firm ran low on money – at a time when interest rates were high and the bank either wouldn't or couldn't help, advising SPL to go to 3i instead.

Financier 3i was a leading international investor that focussed on mid-market private equity, infrastructure and debt management. It invested in supporting people who started, developed, changed and bought businesses. The bank's advice was sound and 3i loaned the firm £300,000 at 17.5% interest, but insisted on an option to buy 20% of SPL for £20,000 with a ten year time limit. SPL met their payments on time and duly repaid the loan. In the meantime Kirklees Chemicals Ltd (part of the SPL group) came on stream in late 1975 and opened in January 1976. This not only met the firm's own needs but, under the leadership of Donald Komrower and a first-class team, sales were developed very rapidly in the UK and throughout Europe. In 1976, with a couple of export awards under its belt, SPL reported revenues in excess of £7,000,000. Just under a quarter of this figure came from over fifty overseas countries. In 1982, when SPL was still a private company, Leslie offered 3i one million pounds to buy back their option, but this was refused.

During the flush of growth in the seventies several new companies were launched. Always looking for a challenge, Leslie found that there was a large market for industrial detergent chemical cleaners. Fully aware that raw material costs and packaging accounted for some 60% of the firm's selling price, Leslie thought that if he could find an area of interest where those costs would be 30% lower, this would be a massive step forward. He and the team felt that main-tenance chemicals would meet this criterion and he was introduced to a man who was working in this field for an American company.

Although sales costs were high, nevertheless the cost of raw materials fell in the brackets SPL set out. Fortunately, with Eric Smith in charge, the company had the technical resources to develop this type of product and in due course Smyth-Morris Chemicals (another company in the group) started life. They quickly built up a sales force of some fifty salesmen and from the beginning all the products were developed in SPL's own laboratory. A small aerosol plant was also included and this gave the firm a wide flexibility of products which from day one proved to be profitable.

The company's first overseas plant, bought in 1978, was located on a three-acre site at Blessington in County Wicklow. This was a small, friendly little company called SPL (Ireland) Ltd. It found a solid niche in a highly independent market with all the research and development (R&D) done at Batley. Regular visits were made in both directions to ensure continuity of quality.

SPL's first two acquisitions, both in the 1970s, were to have a dramatic impact on development although it wasn't realised at the time. One of these was the purchase of Leeds Paint Manufacturing, situated in Morley approximately three miles from the site at Birstall. Leslie had a conversation with the owners of a company called Lancs Tar Distillers, who were wanting to unload what, to them, had been an unsatisfactory purchase a few years earlier. They had a very appealing site and as it dove-tailed easily with SPL, Leslie negotiated the deal. In addition, a couple of months later, a small company called

Wearing a gift of traditional robes on an export trip to West Africa 1971

Allen Walters in London became available through the ill health of the proprietor. SPL had been making emulsion for them for some time, under their own label, for sales to West Africa – it quickly became an export arm of SPL.

More purchasing of property ensued when an old mill in Morley came on the market. This was purchased at an attractive price of £40,000 solely for manufacturing low-cost emulsion. Because SPL's conventional plants were fully employed on a quality range it was felt that a dedicated low-cost plant would be more efficient and cost effective. On one level two large mixing vessels were installed. On the floor below, filling lines were set up which worked well in high productivity and low cost manufacturing. However, about two years after it had come on stream, a fire broke out one morning in the under-drawing of the roof. Old roofs are constructed with tiles which are fastened to tile battens which in turn are secured to the rafters, while new roofs have roofing felt between the tile battens and the rafters, and this is what is referred to as roof under-drawing. Within two hours, the place had completely gone up in flames. The only good news was that the factory was insured for full replacement value as well as loss of profit.

The information was relayed to Leslie who was in London at the time. It came as a great shock to him because the plant had been running extremely well. After things had settled down, Leslie's finance director, Edward Moore, came into Leslie's office and said: "Well, I've just agreed the replacement deal for the plant, the mill and the stock for just over £1 million". Edward had a tempting card up his sleeve which he knew would appeal to his boss. As head of a private company Leslie could place the money in the bank or, he suggested, "There's another option though – you can plough it back into the company for future use." It transpired that at that time Leslie wanted to improve the quality of the Leeds Paint Manufacturing plant so he decided to take Edward's advice.

At a meeting with Eric Smith, Paul Owen and Gordon Bentley, an idea was mooted to design and install a revolutionary, fully computerised plant at the Leeds Paint Manufacturing site. The idea was that raw materials would come in bulk and would be fed into tanks on load-cells. The whole plant was to be controlled by an operator sitting at a computer panel whose job would be to make up

What do we look like today?

This is the main board of Silver Paint and Lacquer (Holdings) Limited.

The efficient management of seven companies, some segmented into various divisions, is a large task. To keep business running smoothly and to plan the path ahead is their task. They have the final decision on matters other than the day-to-day running of individual companies, such as the central financial direction of the group, and group investment policy.

Our main board reviews the activities of all the operating companies in the group, and in some cases is responsible for the setting up of new operations, as in the case of the SPL Pension fund.

The main SPL Board in 1979

1	Stanley S Silver	Sales Director Industrial Division
2	Lawrie Stevens	Sales Director Decorative Division
3	Jack Smethurst	Director
4	Cyril Goldstone	Managing Director Smyth-Morris (Chemicals) Ltd
5	Peter Blake	Consultant
6	Eric Smith	Technical Director
7	Donald W Komrower	Managing Director, Kirklees Chemicals Ltd
8	G Edward Moore	Finance Director
9	Pat Slater	P.A. to L.H. Silver
10	Leslie H Silver	Chairman/Managing Director

the batches simply by pressing a few buttons. With this modern method the first time the paint would be seen was when it came through to the hoppers over the filling lines, after which the lids would be placed on the tins.

By today's values it was a simple and primitive system but by the standards of the 1970s it was ground-breaking and Leslie and his team recovered from their setback. This was perceived not only as a labour-efficient plant but it also proved to be very clean and dust-free. The word soon spread around the industry and shortly thereafter many visitors from all over the world began to arrive to view this radical paint plant. As time went by, the plant was further upgraded, and became increasingly sophisticated.

In the early seventies Leslie joined the Oil and Colour Chemists' Association (OCCA) to discover what else he could learn about modern paint. As a paint manufacturer, Leslie had already joined the Paintmakers Association of Great Britain. He benefited greatly from the many lectures he attended relating to paint, and particularly from the exchange of ideas.

President of the Oil and Colour Chemists' Association 1973-1975

In 1973, Leslie achieved national office as president of OCCA, a post that he held for two years, on one occasion travelling to New Zealand to represent the association and promote the British paint industry. This was followed up in 1978 when Leslie was made president of the Paint Industries Club, which was purely a social club – a post he held for one year.

Another association soon called on his services and one year later, in 1979, he was made president of

President of the
Paintmakers Association
of Great Britain and his
Lady at the Dorchester
Hotel, 1979

the PAGB – Paintmakers Association of Great Britain, holding the post for another year. The main purpose of PAGB was representing the paint industry and the people who worked in it. In 1981 Leslie was once more appointed as annual president of PAGB as well as the Paint Research Association (PRA). It was the first time that any one individual had served as president of all four associations relating to the surface coating industry. The PRA was a research institution with worldwide membership that included manufacturers of paint and its raw materials and major users of paint. Its business was research and service dedicated to the expansion of the technical capabilities and earning capacity of its members.

Although the honorary positions that he occupied at various times gave him personal pleasure, Leslie felt that something should be done to recognise those unsung heroes who, despite long and faithful service to the industry, had not received due acknowledgement. This led him to establish the Silver Medal Award, presented annually to people selected by members of the PAGB.

Receiving the
Queen's
Award for
Export, 1979

In 1979 SPL received the Queen's Award for Export and with the rapid advance of the large DIY superstores, the demand for SPL's private label products increased enormously. The strategy of pile them high, sell them cheap had really paid off.

ENTER KALON

With expansion the old problem returned; once again SPL was running out of space. As the Batley plant was a very old mill and in continuous need of basic repairs, it became virtually impossible to extend. In fact, a journalist from the Financial Times, who came to have a tour of the site, made the cutting remark that 'the nicest part of the plant was the garage'.

In the early 1980s a company called Birstall Carpet Company went into liquidation. The site was in Birstall, a large village in the metropolitan borough of Kirklees in West Yorkshire. Situated roughly six miles south-west of Leeds, it featured a quaint triangular Victorian market place. The site was ideal – located just about a mile from the Batley factory and consisting of some sixty-eight acres with approximately 250,000 square feet of modern single storey factory space. After long drawn-out negotiations, the site was bought for £1.5 million freehold. Another £1 million was lavished on building a new laboratory block as well as another complex for new offices. Leslie decided to apply the techniques he had learned while building the computerised emulsion plant at Morley to the new construction of a super gloss and emulsion plant at Birstall. As far as he was concerned, this was going to be the best ever – constructed of stainless steel throughout with no expense spared. Leslie, with his mastery of manufacturing and retail, was in his element. SPL finally moved into the new Birstall site in 1982 and by this time it had become a strong operator. Annual turnover was some £40 million and profits were approximately £3 million. And through its various subsidiaries, the firm was employing something in the region of 1,000 people.

The Batley site, after a series of changes in ownership, eventually became part of PPG Industries with the factory producing architectural coatings. Sometime later, Leslie was invited back when a boardroom was named after him. One of the changes he quickly noticed was that alcohol was not allowed on the premises, a dramatic change indeed from the days of its previous owners when 'liquid lunches' were the norm.

In the early 1980s the firm acquired Carson Hadfield from Bestobell. Carson had about ten trade centres and a somewhat run-down plant at Mitchum. They employed some good people but the culture was different. In June 1982 Leslie told the workforce at an annual general meeting that "SPL is among the top half dozen British paint manufacturers so let's take it onwards and upwards." Having completed the re-organisation of the group following the Carson Hadfield's take-over, he was pleased to report that all companies in the group were performing in line with their budgets for 1982.

He took the view that "the Board is ready and willing to invest capital in all of our sites to ensure their top line performance and efficiency. We want them to be the best." However, he added, changes would have to be made because the country was still in the middle of an economic recession. After adjustments had been made, Leslie was apologetic but optimistic. As he said at the time: "We hope these changes and the job losses that have regrettably been necessary have enabled us to maintain full-time employment, and to assist us in meeting our markets efficiently. We hope also that they have occurred with the minimum of hurt to those concerned."

Leslie thought that the upturn would eventually arrive and that when it did "we will be ready with plenty of capacity to meet increased business." At that time Leslie felt that being 'big in business' was both a tremendous challenge and a responsibility – it was essential that the group serve all of its customers with maximum efficiency and courtesy. "Without them we have no business", he stated. "They must all, big and small, be treated like royalty" and to achieve this he depended on SPL employees.

The companies in the group at that time were Silver Paints, Leeds Paints, Kirklees Chemicals, Smyth Morris Chemicals, SPL Ireland, Allen Walters, Horgen Chemicals, Carson Hadfield and Always Transport, a distribution company.

Leslie now got to grips with a problem that had been troubling him for some time. With the increase in the number of companies joining the Group, he had noticed that a form of snobbery had gradually appeared, and he was having none of that. Directors from SPL tended to act, subconsciously, in a superior manner to other subsidiary directors. Leslie felt this was wrong because, he reasoned, they were all on the same team and teamwork was the cement that held the whole enterprise together. He accordingly felt it necessary to revitalise the family spirit.

Leslie came to the conclusion that there was a need to form a holding company as an umbrella organisation, but what name should be used for it? He had always disliked Silver Paint and Lacquer Company as a name, and at one of the twice-weekly directors' lunches, which always involved an element of liquid refreshment, Leslie asked for suggestions for a new company name. Much hilarity ensued while brief consideration was given to all sorts of crazy names, none of which held any real appeal. Then, out of the blue, Ces Butler, who was quietly doing the Yorkshire Post crossword, piped up: "What about Kalon?" "What about Kalon?", Leslie responded tartly. Ces tapped his pencil against the open page. "Well, it's a clue in today's crossword and it's an ancient Greek name that means 'for the greater good'." The room suddenly fell silent. Everyone was deep in thought, and Leslie was the first to speak.

"Well, it's a pleasant enough word, much snappier than Silver Paints, that's for sure – and it rolls off the tongue easily. In addition, with just five letters, it is easy to recall – just like Dulux."

Ces put down his newspaper and Leslie said, "Actually, it's brilliant! Let's go with that – Kalon it is." And the die was cast.

෴ ෴ ෴

By this time, the firm had been approached on many occasions with offers to buy, but these offers had always been rejected. However, Leslie was approaching retirement age so the future of the family's finances and the company's prospects became a big issue. After much consideration, he decided that a flotation on the stock exchange was the best way forward and he engaged S G Warburg as advisors. At that time, the firm was turning over roughly £60 million, with profits of between £4 million and £4.5 million. Warburg's made it clear that unless the company was showing a clear upward trend in turnover and profits, it would get a low market rating and the value of the new shares, so far as the family was concerned, would be disappointing.

For some weeks the discussions continued and, eventually, it was decided that a reverse into an already listed company, with Kalon taking control, would be the best option. Leyland Paints was proposed as a suitable candidate for this purpose. It was less than half the size of Kalon and had been experiencing all kinds of problems – many of which emerged after the deal was done. However, the key point was that it was available.

Leslie recalled that as soon as talks were started, Leyland's share price, previously in the doldrums, suddenly took off. At the level at which it settled it was totally unattractive so Leslie walked away. This resulted in Leyland's price collapsing and things went quiet for a few weeks.

A couple of months went by until one of Leyland's top people came to Leslie's house with a deal that seemed reasonably attractive. Leslie accepted and the deal was done quickly and neatly and the family and other shareholders in Kalon were happy. Kalon now had control of a listed company and stockbrokers Cazenove placed 30% of Kalon shares on the market. The board was restructured and Kalon eventually settled down to life as a public limited company.

New kinds of problems inevitably arose, but so far as Kalon and Leslie were concerned, this was the end of a chapter in a history dating back to the formation of Silver Paint and Lacquer Co Ltd.

Kalon entered 1985 with a degree of confidence. The new paint factory at Birstall was slowly coming on stream and among other innovations came the launch of a new solid paint, competing very effectively with ICI. Leslie thought it was "a good product that proved to be quite a challenge to our technical and production staff, but a challenge that they were well fitted to meet." The previous year had finished reasonably strongly with sales just a bit short of budget and profits similar to the year before. Kalon saw a few changes in both its paint and chemical divisions but Leslie thought it was particularly gratifying to see the increased level of co-operation between various warehouses and sales forces and he felt that it "pointed to good vibes for the future."

It was in 1985 that Leslie's younger brother Stanley, who had been with the company almost since its inception, decided to step down and retire. Stanley, married to Ruth Morgan, felt that it was time to move on and apart from pursuing other things that interested him, wanted to spend time with his wife and family. Leslie said he and 'the firm' would miss him.

Following some changes in the Kalon Group structure, Leslie's son-in-law Oded Brosh, was appointed Group Operations Director. In addition to his purchasing responsibilities, he was put in charge of warehousing, distribution and transport.

It became apparent that the close co-operation which existed previously had now been extended across the Kalon Group as a whole and had already resulted in the initiation of major ideas resulting in significant cost savings to the company. Andy Rodgers, Kalon's transport and distribution manager, Ron Lovett, Carson Hadfield transport manager and Terry Tweddle, transport manager for Penetone Horgan, had already worked to provide excellent services to their individual companies. With further close co-operation under Oded Brosh, it was hoped that the principle of customer service, which had been a major factor in building Kalon, would not only be maintained but improved upon as the group continued to expand.

However, after the Leyland Paints acquisition, problems soon began to emerge. Leslie discovered that the due diligence performed on Leyland had left much to be desired. In particular, prior to the takeover, Leyland's stocks had been inflated. Leslie called a meeting in the boardroom of all senior staff where he and his directors explained the current trading conditions in graphic detail. Speaking straight from the shoulder, he gave out the message loud and clear. Leslie told them that at a time when the home market continued to shrink, "we are not content to run faster to maintain our position. We need to get out and fight for a bigger share."

Competition was the lifeblood of the Kalon Group and each subsidiary company carried the responsibility for its own success. In typical fashion, Leslie spelt out his message: "We have no time for frills and no room for passengers. While the salesman might superficially appear to be a more crucial position than the order-taker, when the salesman is successful he relies on every other part of the organisation to provide a super service."

The £6 million he had spent in Birstall was an indication of the investment that the group was making to ensure success in the future. Surveying the market in general, Leslie thought that any changes would have to be evolutionary rather than revolutionary. It was difficult to recover from dramatic changes, he maintained.

Like all paint manufacturers, Kalon Group had seen a reduction of its overall profit margin during the previous four years, even though the company had expanded its sphere of operations. So far as the future was concerned, Leslie promised that they would take advantage of opportunities as they presented themselves and no doubt continue to diversify, evolving in line with the industry itself.

Leslie always felt that his 'big mistake' was to appoint, as chief executive, Leyland Paints' James MacDonald, a non-practising barrister. According to Leslie, he was naturally concerned to preserve the reputation of Leyland Paints and accordingly, as was subsequently discovered, covered up many things that should have been exposed. His speciality was in stretching meetings out unnecessarily which caused much friction and irritability.

A new finance director had also been appointed. He was called Payne and, in Leslie's view, certainly lived up to his name – he turned out to be something of a disaster.

With these problems mounting so quickly after the flotation, Leslie decided to have a clear-out and brought in consultants from Robson Rhodes, resulting in the firing of both the chief executive officer and the new finance director in the same morning. Mike Hennessey saw the announcement for a CEO in the Financial Times and immediately applied for the job and was successful.

In 1987, Kalon suffered its first-ever loss, which amounted to over £1 million. Hennessey did a good job in cost-cutting and the firm rapidly returned to a reasonable level of profitability, although he sold Smyth Morris and Kirklees Chemicals, which in Leslie's view was a mistake. Unfortunately, Leslie never hit it off with Hennessey. In his view, he was a first-rate, short-term cost-cutter, but lacked the vision for long-term company growth.

∾ ∾ ∾

On 6 May 1987, Kalon commenced operations at its new 60-acre site on Huddersfield Road in Birstall, the nerve centre for the now hugely enlarged original paint business which that year celebrated its fortieth anniversary.

HRH The Duke of Gloucester performed the official opening and showed great interest in the newly-extended range of solid emulsions, confessing that he always had a problem with paint landing on his specs when he was painting a ceiling. The Duke arrived with his motorcade from Leeds Bradford Airport. The Deputy Lord Lieutenant introduced members of the official welcome party, who were proudly waiting at the factory steps which were decked with a fantastic floral display in honour of the occasion. The Duke showed great delight in the skid resistance testing procedures he saw in the Enfield Road Marking laboratory and revealed that the thermoplastic raised white lines were a constant fear to him when he was riding his motorbike in the centre of London. The Duke was taken on a tour of the laboratories and stopped to help trainee technical assistant Elaine Jackson with her task of colour-matching paint samples. He also showed an interest in quality control and asked manager Roy Flynn

Opening of the new Birstall factory. Leslie with HRH the Duke of Gloucester talking to employees

Sheila Silver greets the Duke of Gloucester, watched by Leslie and the MP for Kirklees, Elizabeth Peacock

to explain some of the procedures undertaken to ensure consistent product quality. Technicians in the department had recently raised £50 for a local hospice through the introduction of a swear box – but on this occasion no one slipped up while the Duke was around.

The 180,000 square foot factory, controlled by micro processors from the central computer room, was in full swing when the Duke arrived. He witnessed production operations, including the filling lines, before moving through to the export packing department for a tour conducted by manager Sam Haigh. Further members of the staff and board, together with some of their wives and family, were presented to the Duke during his visit to the ground floor sales area in the new prestige office complex.

Architect Martin Joyce, of Martin Joyce Associates, discussed some of the building's design points with the Duke, who was himself a qualified architect. He was highly amused to learn that the flat roof construction had caused few problems other than a small leak over the chairman's desk which had been quickly repaired.

The Duke paid tribute to Kalon for the redevelopment of the site which he said "had now been given a rebirth." He also praised the company's continued efforts in the technological improvement of paint to offer better products and colour ranges without a corresponding increase in prices.

"Paint now represents especially good value for the do-it-yourself brigade", he said, adding that "I hope they will take advantage of the extra value offered from this modern factory." With personal experience of dealing with clients, he was interested to know what Kalon had been like as customers. Mr Joyce replied instantly: "Without a doubt – excellent, of course."

Leslie invited the Duke to honour the firm with the unveiling of a commemorative plaque which was situated in the reception area of the most modern paint factory in Europe. Before the Duke departed, Leslie asked him to sign the visitors' book in which he inscribed: "Richard – May 6, 1987." In its own modest way, history had been made and recorded.

By 1991 Leslie was past retirement age and he felt that it was time for him and the Kalon Group to move on in different directions, although he would still retain his major shareholding. So at Christmas 1991 he retired.

In retrospect, Leslie often asked himself why he and the firm had survived when so many others had failed. In 1950, the Hull and Yorkshire Paint-Makers Association had about fifty members. Hull was the home of paint-making in Yorkshire although the oldest company was located in Ripon. By the start of the new millennium, very few firms had survived and many had been taken over. Leslie always thought that Kalon's strengths were its people and its team spirit.

"Our relationships at all levels were warm, honest and straightforward and that is an important factor in any business", he said at a workforce dinner. "People expressed their views freely without fear of recrimination and also our organisational structure enabled us to make decisions quickly – we became famous for our corridor meetings." A conversation in passing often resulted in a decision being taken and acted upon in an informal manner without wasting time, and this proved to be a procedure that worked extremely well.

On reflection, Leslie always maintained that what made the firm successful was a consistent attitude towards people. "I think it made us different from other companies. We had a relaxed, informal style and everyone in the company was important, respected and a key member of the team and easy to talk to", he said at his farewell party.

Five

Hard Work
Brings its Rewards

I N 1982, LESLIE WAS AWARDED the Order of the British Empire and two years later named Yorkshire Businessman of the Year. Pat Slater, Leslie's secretary, had received a phone call one day from the Department of Trade and Industry asking for Leslie's biography as they wanted to nominate him for an OBE.

Deep down Leslie regarded himself as republican and believed that the best kind of government was one in which supreme power was vested in the electorate. He was highly patriotic, believing that if one lived and worked in a country and engaged with its cultural activities then one should be loyal to its ideals, but his views on the royal family were ambivalent and somewhat at odds with his republican leanings.

He had already met various members of the royal family. Prince Philip, at a Jewish charity function in London, had impressed him enormously and he was heartened to see him wearing a *yarmulke*, the traditional Jewish skull cap, as well as speaking warmly of the state of Israel.

Professor Leslie Wagner, former vice-chancellor of two universities and chancellor of Derby University, recalls a charity dinner when he was sitting at the same table as Leslie and the conversation turned to the monarchy. Leslie was arguing vociferously for republicanism, saying that "the whole royalty set-up was a diversion and a waste of money." His protest was interrupted by the master of ceremonies who called the guests to order and invited Leslie on stage to propose the loyal toast, which he did most eloquently. Returning to his table with a wry smile on his face, he took up the strands of his argument and continued to argue the case for the abolition of the monarchy.

Leslie was humbled, honoured and secretly excited that his name had been put forward for the OBE. It came at a time when Anita's health was deteriorating and the news gave her a great boost, so Leslie had no hesitation in accepting. The whole family was thrilled when the letter finally arrived saying that the Queen had decided to award him with an OBE in the Queen's Birthday Honours of 1982. In the winter of that year, Leslie and Anita journeyed to London with Hilary, Jane and Mark to attend the award-giving ceremony at Buckingham Palace.

To his surprise he found the occasion a profoundly moving experience and was delighted with how well organised it all was. Because his surname came towards the end of the alphabet Leslie and the family had quite a long wait before he met the Queen, but this turned out to be advantageous because they were quite happy to soak in the ambience whilst waiting. He remarked to the family afterwards that he 'would have been a hypocrite' if he didn't admit he enjoyed the occasion.

He found the Queen to be most amiable and well-informed. To Leslie the award, while it was a huge personal honour, also reflected

Hilary, Anita, Leslie and Jane at Buckingham Palace after Leslie received the OBE

on SPL and recognised the achievements the company had made over the years in the industry. It also gave provided recognition to Anita whose support and love for him and the company was second to none. The Queen asked Leslie if he enjoyed his job and his reply was in the affirmative, "Indeed, I do, ma'am." Suddenly, his favourite colour was royal blue.

Afterwards Leslie took the family for a slap-up lunch at the Ritz. His visits to the Palace would continue in the future as he enjoyed attending two or three garden parties.

The occasion of the OBE award was also very poignant on a personal level because Anita's health was a cause of great concern. At one point, doctors had advised her not to travel. She had undergone heart surgery at Leeds General Infirmary some years earlier, although it had proved to be 'a bit of a trauma'. A recurrence of symptoms that included pain and discomfort prompted her to seek further consultations, with the result that another operation was advised. Not wanting to have the operation in Leeds because of dissatisfaction with some of the surgeons, she was recommended by a friend to consult a Harley Street surgeon. Leslie decided to take her down to London in January 1983. But matters took a turn for the worse and to the family's distress she did not survive the operation and died in the operating theatre on 31 January 1983.

It was a great consolation for Leslie and the family to know that Anita, who had been hugely instrumental in helping him to build up the business, had been there to see their life-work duly recognised by the monarch. Leslie and Anita had enjoyed an exciting and successful marriage of some thirty-seven years duration and after her death he was to enter a dark and stressful period of his life, sometimes causing him to cry when he least expected it.

Shortly after Anita's death, Leslie complained of chest pains and consulted a specialist. He had been a heavy smoker ever since his days in the RAF. One of the downsides of flying was a rigid no-smoking rule which placed regular smokers under stress. When a crew landed back at base there was an inevitable period of waiting to be picked up, usually by a transport team from the WAAF. Consequently, the first thing most airmen did was to light up, chiefly to relax and unwind. For the most part, in those days, smoking was the norm. If one didn't smoke then one wasn't in the loop.

At the time of Anita's death Leslie was smoking cigars, and when his consultant heard how long his smoking habit had lasted he said: "A smoker for some forty years, eh? I don't suppose there is much point then in me telling you that you need to stop now, is there?" Leslie looked up and enquired: "Do you mean my smoking is the cause of my respiratory problems?" The consultant nodded. "Let's put it this way, smoking is certainly a contributory factor."

Leslie reached into his jacket pocket and brought out a nearly-full packet of cigars and without hesitation tossed them straight into the consultant's waste paper basket. That was to be the last time Leslie ever smoked – a prime example of his determination and indomitable willpower.

A DIFFERENT COAT OF PAINT

In 1976, art lover Dr Jeffrey Sherwin, chairman of Leeds Leisure Services, invited Yorkshire sculptor Henry Moore and his wife Mary to Leeds. Dr Sherwin planned to build an extension to Leeds City Art Gallery as a tribute to Moore. At that point in time, the city's art gallery was becoming somewhat unsafe – indeed, so much so that one of the rooms was supported on pit-props and the staircase was thought to be insecure. As a result, the art gallery was virtually closed.

There had been a scheme to put a lattice-work around the gallery to hold it together and put the heavy sculpture on the roof, but that proved to be too expensive and impractical. In spite of many appeals addressed to locals and to the higher echelons of government, only £20,000 was allocated by the relevant governmental department, which was headed by Michael Heseltine. Listening to a discussion about these problems at one meeting, Sherwin had the idea of building out over the existing frontage and paying for it by building a pub into the basement. Everybody laughed and the idea was shelved. When the Conservatives won another term in office a year later, Sherwin once again put forward the idea to his colleagues on the city council and once again everybody laughed.

Undeterred, Sherwin used his own money to hire an architect to draw up a sketch plan which was judged to be cost effective by the city. The council came to the conclusion that with the right level of rent paid by the pub lessee, the proposal would work. However, the rest of the gallery would still be unsafe and Leisure Services would need to raise funds for a major renovation. Sherwin's suggestion was to package up the gallery into sponsored units and to offer rooms to be named after their sponsors in return for a large donation. What he envisaged to help the enterprise along was the advice of 'a first generation millionaire' and he told his committee that he had identified just the man.

Although he didn't know Leslie personally, he certainly knew him by repute and of his willingness to help the city. So he invited Leslie to a sandwich-lunch at Temple Newsam House with himself and Robert Rowe who held the post of art gallery director from 1958 to 1983. Meetings were always held in Temple Newsam's original dining room, often with a log fire crackling in the grate. The room was rather large and doubled up as Rowe's office. According to Rowe's draft manuscript, 'Artefacts and Figures: an Account of Stewardship', currently resting in the Brotherton Library, both men took to Leslie at once. Rowe described him as 'big, bluff and obviously good-hearted'. However, as Rowe had noted, "He soon admitted that he knew next to nothing about art but clearly this confession caused him no heartache." After lunch, with a drop of wine added for good measure, Rowe and Sherwin put the sponsorship proposal before Leslie. They explained the proposal and all of its complications but found it somewhat difficult to persuade him that all they sought, at least at that stage, was his advice. They described the idea of offering nine galleries to sponsors who, in return for a significant amount of money, could have their names emblazoned in the gallery of their choice or over its entrance.

Leslie was confident they had a 'highly saleable commodity' and, after some debate, the three decided that £30,000 was a reasonable figure to request. As the first meeting was purely to seek advice, both Rowe and Sherwin followed it up by accepting an invitation to lunch with Leslie at his factory. They realised this would be the time to ask for money – not always an easy task – but were relieved to discover that this would not be necessary. To their delight Leslie had given the matter a lot of thought and was most enthusiastic, telling them that he and his wife Anita would be happy to sponsor a south-facing top floor room in Leeds Art Gallery, with their names above its access doors, leading to the open-air sculpture terrace. And he was happy to offer the first £30,000. Apart from this, Leslie considered that not much had been made of the Henry Moore angle which he felt could become one of the city's greatest assets and he gave further advice on how to market the appeal.

In his diaries Robert Rowe penned: "I have gone into some detail over the Leslie Silver connection because, looking back, I can see that not only were his views and help practical in every sense, but he gave us confidence and backing for a tricky part of our campaign, at a time when we were feeling the strain and might have gone off the boil."

In 1979, the Henry Moore Foundation announced plans for the establishment of the Henry Moore Centre for the Study of Sculpture in Leeds City Art Gallery, resulting one year later in Henry Moore laying the foundation stone. And so it came to pass that on 26 November 1982, Her Majesty the Queen opened the renovated Leeds City Art Gallery and the Moore Sculpture Gallery. After some refurbishment, the Leslie and Anita Silver Art Gallery was opened without an official launch and with as little fuss as possible – a process of which Leslie, naturally, heartily approved.

HM The Queen with Leslie and Anita at the opening of the new City Art Gallery building, 1982

THE NOT ALWAYS BEAUTIFUL GAME

Leslie, passionate about the beautiful game ever since his childhood in the East End, had been a Leeds United supporter since his arrival in the city. He thought that to be involved in any aspect of the sport was a rewarding and exciting experience. As a child, he went with his uncles to watch Arsenal play at Highbury and became hooked on the game. He'd played football at school but never thought of himself as anything but a gifted amateur.

When he relocated to Leeds changing allegiance to Leeds United had not been difficult. As a Leeds resident he felt an affinity not only to the club but to the city which had welcomed him and which he had grown to love. He had visited Elland Road to watch a friendly game towards the end of the 1948/49 season when Leeds United played Queen of the South. The regular Leeds centre half was Tom Holley but, due to injury, he was not playing. Instead a young lad called John Charles was brought in as his replacement.

Leslie enquired: "What kind of idiot would play a kid like that against a huge Scottish international?" However, as it turned out Charles played an inspired game and easily snuffed out any threat. The upshot was that Holley was never again to play for Leeds and Leslie was to add another player to his list of favourites. Charles subsequently took on the role of striker, going on to enter the record books for goals scored in a season when he struck a phenomenal 42 goals during the 1953/54 season.

William John Charles was born on 27 December 1931 in Swansea. He was equally adept at centre forward or centre back. He was never cautioned or sent off during his entire career. Leslie came to hold the view that Charles was the greatest player ever to play for Leeds United and many decades later, when Leslie became associated with Leeds Metropolitan University, he was instrumental in Charles – the 'gentle giant' – being awarded an honorary degree.

However, the John Charles glory days were long past. It was now 1981 and a bleak period in the club's history with its record of hooliganism and racialism. At that time the club represented the worst aspects of English football. Leeds was a club on the downward slope after the glory years with Don .

Manny Cussins had joined the LU Board of directors in 1961 and served as chairman from 1972. One evening in April 1982, at a charity function in the home of Leeds financial entrepreneur Arnold Ziff, Leslie's neighbour, Manny was networking and desperately looking for investment. He approached Leslie and said: "I hear you're a football fan and particularly interested in Leeds United. Would you like to join United's board?" Ever the businessman, Leslie cautiously enquired: "What is it going to cost me?" to which Cussins replied "Absolutely nothing."

As it turned out that was not entirely true because, even though what Cussins was after was money to be loaned to the club to buy players, the capital was to be paid back to lenders but without interest. Leslie subsequently did some digging and discovered that the interest payments on the money borrowed to pay for new signings Peter Barnes and Kenny Burns had left Leeds United on the verge of bankruptcy.

Later that evening Leslie discussed the proposition with Anita who was not in favour. He was at a stage in life where he was making money, and making it in a big way, and both had worked extremely hard to attain it. Both he and Anita had come from humble beginnings and started married life on a Leeds council estate and now, at last, they were able to live a life of ease, style and luxury. Anita thought that if Leslie joined the LU board and became involved in the finances of the club, their lifestyle could be swiftly altered. Leslie, on the other hand, saw the proposal as another challenge and after much deliberation he joined the board later that year, putting in £2 million by way of a loan – which was enough to buy an Australian full-back.

Hooliganism had haunted Leeds United since the 1975 Paris riot when so-called 'fans' tore up seats at the European Cup final. Leeds had a reputation as a club of thugs, but Leslie discovered that the problems were not confined to the pitch-side.

The club had 2,000 shares, widely-held since the 1920s. After Leslie joined there was a rights issue worth an additional £250,000. Manny Cussins, Peter Gilman and Leslie each took up £50,000 of new shares and other board members took up smaller amounts. The board now held majority control but there was another problem looming – crowds had whittled down to a sad 13,000.

The location of Elland Road was in principle a huge advantage. Exempt from the problems associated with cramped inner-city sites, the ground was in open land, close to two motorways yet within walking distance from the city centre. The board sold the stadium to Leeds City Council to wipe out debts of £2 million and put the club into a similar situation to continental teams of renting a municipal facility. Leslie felt deeply that the deal committed the council and the board to treat the club as part of the city's culture. "If you lose football then something goes out of people's lives", Leslie was to say to one national newspaper.

In 1983, Manny Cussins decided to call it a day and retired as chairman of Leeds United. A year later, Leslie took over the chairmanship. In his new role, Leslie discovered a developed sense of civic duty and pride and found the new challenge taking on epic proportions.

With his mind in business mode, he decided firstly to restructure the finances by introducing new money by way of a share issue and selling the freehold to the city council with a commitment to work with local community activities. The aim was clear. It was essential the club play a positive role in improving community facilities in the south west section of the city. Subsequently, over a period of years, steps were taken to achieve these objectives and Leslie was nothing if not forward thinking. These included the recruitment of a number of black players which immediately eliminated racial chanting and abusive comments at games. All players were bound by contract, if requested, to give seven hours a week to community service in schools and youth clubs. It was as if Leslie wanted to echo L.S. Lowry's great painting of 'Going To The Match' by making a football game attendance an essential family occasion.

With this in mind, a family stand facility was established, as well as a fully staffed crèche which became available at every game and during the week. Local residents warmed to the idea. To enhance the sporting spirit Leslie also introduced exchange facilities with other club's family groups. This enabled parents and children to enjoy club facilities at each game in complete safety and with peace of mind.

Amenities were also provided during the week for the unemployed. The aim was to improve their employment prospects by teaching certain basic skills such as secretarial expertise and in some cases returning to basics and instructing people how to read and write. This project, formed in conjunction with the Apex Trust, fulfilled a desperate need in the area. In addition, two or three times a week, the facilities were made available for local women to attend aerobic classes. These were women who, by necessity, normally had to stay at home to look after their families.

The introduction of an identity card scheme and an all-ticket facility for away fixtures soon eradicated the worst of the hooligan issues, while the sale of Elland Road to Leeds City Council brought financial stability. It was felt that United could just about pay its way but, sooner or later, the issue had to be addressed that there was no money available to buy quality players. Furthermore, the club was in desperate need of a competent new manager.

Warm memories still remained of the glory days of Don Revie, a dream manager if ever there was one. It was Revie who had famously declared that 'Leeds United is a lump of ground – it's the team that matters.' Leslie was now obliged to test out several managers in the hope of discovering someone even remotely as good as Revie. This proved to be a most unrewarding experience.

In June 1969, Revie had paid £165,000 to Leicester City for Allan Clarke's services. Clarke scored twenty-six goals in his first season, earning him the nickname Sniffer because of his predatory instincts in front of goal. Clarke made his mark at LU as a player before moving on to Barnsley as player-manager in June 1978. A year later, after Barnsley finished in mid-table, Leeds United invited him to come back to the club as manager in 1980. However, the move didn't go according to plan because at the end of the 1980/81 season Leeds United finished ninth. The following year they were relegated and Clarke was sacked in June 1982 at the end of the season.

His replacement at Leeds was his mate Eddie Gray, but unfortunately he also proved unable to improve performances. Edwin 'Eddie' Gray was a cultured winger in the classic mould who had become an integral member of the United team in the sixties and seventies. He took over as player-manager in 1982 following the White's relegation from the First Division. However, after failing to gain promotion from the Second Division (now, perversely, called the Championship), Gray, in 1985, was also given the sack. Leslie was to confess that sacking Gray, who he thought was a great guy, was his hardest decision during his time as chairman.

Leslie then turned his attention to Billy Bremner who was brought in as manager. Bremner had been a world-class footballer most noted for his captaincy of the Leeds United team of the 1960s and 1970s. He was voted United's greatest player of all time and the nine-foot-high statue outside the south east corner of Elland Road, created by Leeds-born sculptor Frances Segelman in 1999, has since become a famous Leeds landmark. Records show, however, that Bremner was more at home kicking the ball as a player than in planning team strategy for forthcoming matches. Sadly the team never regained promotion while Bremner was manager, although it lost a play-off final to Charlton Athletic in 1987 and reached the FA Cup semi-finals in the same season.

In 1988, as Leeds United sat near the bottom of the Second Division and was struggling to avoid relegation to the Third Division, Leslie hated the Second Division and early in the 1988/89 campaign he sacked Bremner and informed the LU board that a replacement was needed.

Jack Marjason, who was on the board, told Leslie that he understood there was a dispute involving the Sheffield Wednesday manager, Howard Wilkinson who had led the Owls into the First Division in 1984, and his chairman at the club. Wilkinson had been lumbered with the nickname Sergeant Bilko, an allusion to the behaviour of the fictional US television sitcom character Sergeant Bilko as played memorably by Phil Silvers. Marjason suggested the unsettled Wilkinson might be tempted to come to Leeds, but Leslie didn't really believe that the manager of one of the country's top clubs would ever contemplate such a move. Marjason told Leslie: 'Nothing ventured, nothing gained' and persuaded Leslie to contact the Sheffield Wednesday chairman.

Leslie decided to phone the chairman at seven the next morning. Leslie believed in putting his cards firmly on the table and told the chairman that he understood Wilkinson was uncomfortable at Wednesday and asked whether it would be acceptable to approach him about a job at Leeds United. It may or may not have been due to the early hour, but to Leslie's surprise the chairman gave him permission to speak to Wilkinson who was promptly invited to meet Leslie at his Kalon office in Birstall.

Wilkinson, a strong-minded individual, came one Thursday afternoon. Leslie gave him a warm welcome and, looking for liquid inspiration, opened a vintage bottle of whisky. After the niceties were observed there was to be no further beating about the bush and Leslie asked him directly if he would be interested in joining Leeds United. Wilkinson thought for a few seconds before responding in the affirmative. "What do you know about the club?" Leslie asked. Wilkinson then proceeded to reel off an inventory of every player's strengths and weaknesses. Leslie was impressed but also thoughtful. He leaned forward and enquired: "Tell me Howard, have you been angling for this job?" Wilkinson answered the question with a question of his own and asked Leslie about his ambitions for Leeds United. Leslie quickly replied: "My ambition is to get us out of the Second Division, I'm sick of it."

"How would you like it done?" asked Wilkinson. "We can get out the quick way or the slow way." Leslie said he preferred the former and enquired how long it would take. "Mr Silver, you know about the paint industry, do you not, that's your business after all. Well, you see football is my business." Wilkinson asked for £2 million to rebuild the team and revolutionise the club. Without hesitation Leslie responded: "Howard, you've got it."

The outcome of that Thursday afternoon meeting was the establishment of an enduring relationship between the two men, helped undoubtedly by a bottle of very high quality Scotch.

For Wilkinson, a tough-minded Yorkshireman, the devil was in the detail and everything had to be pre-planned. His future teams were ruthlessly selected and meticulously drilled with military precision. When he arrived in Leeds, the eighth manager in roughly fifteen years, the club was in danger of dropping into the Third Division. He rapidly parted ways with the coach, Norman Hunter, and took down any photographs of the Revie era. The club was in 'a sorry mess', he declared. It didn't even own its ground or the neglected training ground and it had grotty changing rooms.

Wilkinson regarded the job as a sacred mission and went on to save the club from relegation. Leeds United was promoted back to the First Division in 1989-90 and went on to win the League title in the 1991/92 season.

The name Leeds United was to become synonymous with Leslie Silver and one of Leslie's most durable memories relates to 1992 after winning the League title in the same year that the Premiership was launched. The team played in the Charity Shield at Wembley, beating

Chairman Leslie Silver, Directors Bill Fotherby and Peter Gilman and Captain Gordon Strachan with the Championship Cup, 2 May 1992

Victory parade on Briggate, 3 May 1992, after Leeds United won the Championship

Liverpool 4-3, and Eric Cantona scored a hat trick. Leslie walked out on to the balcony and the Liverpool and Leeds fans were walking peacefully together down Wembley Way. Turning to Liverpool chairman David Moores, he said: "Now this is what football is all about."

As for Wilkinson, Leslie always thought he was Leeds United's best manager since Don Revie. He brought in the likes of Gordon Strachan, Gary McAllister and Tony Yeboah on a shoe-string budget. When he finally bid farewell eight years later, United had a magnificent stadium, had its own state-of-the-art academy training facility and financially were very solid indeed. Wilkinson had waved his sword-edged magic wand.

In April 1996, with fourteen years in charge under his belt, Leslie announced his resignation as chairman of Leeds United. He was still the largest shareholder in the club and Leslie intended to sell his 33% stake in the long term which would offer potential for a prospective bidder to buy a controlling interest in the club. With his departure, the club lost an extraordinary chairman and visionary. Leslie's family constantly asked him why he bothered about football and his reply was always the same. It was because he had been a huge fan and passionate about the club from the day he walked into Elland Road after being demobbed in 1947. At the time he was merely a supporter on the terraces, a young man gambling his RAF gratuity, as well as money loaned from members of his family, on a new business venture.

As Leslie noted when asked why he had taken on the job of chairman when the club was at such a low ebb: "I could afford it, through luck and endeavour in my business. It was money I had earned." But what Leslie had inherited from Manny Cussins, after he approached him to take control, was a club whose supporters, in the words of a High Court judge, "risked taking the country to the devil." The judge made his comments after Leeds hooligans had intimidated Crown witnesses into refusing to give evidence – and many experts were pointing to Manny's resignation at a time when supporters were mouthing threats towards him.

The reason Leslie would be written into the history books would undoubtedly include his tackling head-on the problem of hooliganism that had infiltrated the terraces, as well as his re-drafting of the club's responsibility towards the wider community.

NEVER TOO LATE FOR AN EDUCATION

In 1987 Mrs Thatcher's government decided that, because the majority of local councils were dominated by the Labour Party, the money for higher education should go directly from government to the education centre itself. It was accordingly left to the then Leeds Polytechnic to implement the elements of the Education Reform Act 1988, which provided for the independence of polytechnics from local authority control.

One evening George Mudie, Leader of Leeds City Council, who was an old friend of Leslie's through a shared passion for Leeds United, phoned him to extend an invitation to become chairman of the formation committee of Leeds Polytechnic, with the aim of converting the organisation into a format appropriate for its new powers. Leslie was sceptical. "George, that's an impossibility. You do realise I left school at fourteen, so what do I know about education? You're speaking to the wrong man."

George chuckled and replied: "Hold on a minute Leslie, we are not looking for an academic; what we are searching for is a solid, experienced business man, someone who is erudite about commerce and can handle finances sensibly."

He pointed out that Leslie's enormously successful business record would stand him in good stead for the job, which would be to oversee the finances of the organisation. "I'll tell you what, Leslie. Try it out for six months, and then if you don't like the job just walk away – no harm done."

Weighing the pros and cons, Leslie realised how important it was to seize the day and grab the opportunities that were offered. On the other hand, he was moving into unknown territory and growing closer to the 'establishment' was not exactly a priority. Nevertheless, he soon succumbed to Mudie's advice and, in 1989, Leslie proved to be the person, agreeable to all sides, who was chosen to chair the new organisation.

His friend Professor Leslie Wagner thought he was the ideal person for the job. He considered Leslie to be intellectually sharp, shrewd and very perceptive. Attempting to dispel any personal shortcomings his friend may have felt about himself, he told Leslie that although it arguably shouldn't work, he certainly felt that it would. "You will soon learn to gloss over difficulties, or to assume some issue was too complex for you to understand."

Leslie accepted the post with typical modesty and, as anticipated, attacked the work with his customary zeal. An added fillip was that he got on extremely well with the committee, which comprised of twelve to fifteen people, including the vice chancellor, staff members and one young person elected by the students themselves. To Leslie's surprise, if to no one else's, he took to the job like a duck to water. His remit entailed the utilisation of the capital money and funds received from the government, as well as finding ways of obtaining more cash at a reasonable rate of interest, which in the 1980s was something of a tall order.

One central issue that needed to be addressed quickly became apparent to Leslie. He was appalled at the amount of money that had been borrowed by the Polytechnic at very high rates of interest. One of the lenders was based in Cardiff and the people involved were keen to continue to lend money to the new universities knowing full well that the people they were lending to would not be there long enough to be held accountable. They were fully aware that the management would change and that the debt would continue to grow and be a risk-free, profitable source of income for them well into the future.

There was one occasion when the Polytechnic decided to build a new block of student accommodation and the finance company was pushing to lend more money. When it contacted Leslie to negotiate the deal, there was undoubtedly an element of shock and surprise when Leslie announced that the Polytechnic would not be pursuing another loan. He told them that his strategy would be to use the cash they had in the bank until it ran out, and then to borrow more money from the bank until the time came when the next set of grants were received from the government. Leslie felt this was a plan that most businesses would endorse and eventually it did turn out to work satisfactorily, thus proving, if proof was needed, that his business acumen was vital in aiding the Polytechnic to become financially stable.

Leslie's chairing of meetings might best be described as brisk. Coming from the private sector where time was money, and even taking into account his love of a good argument, he could not comprehend why everybody talked so much at the meetings. After the Vice-Chancellor arrived a meeting would commence and Leslie would peruse the agenda and, for example, pick out Item 4, the Finance Report.

"Anybody want to say anything on this?" Leslie would ask those present, waving the agenda sheet in the air. He would wait a good three seconds and then, if no one intervened, would say: "Fine, so that's agreed then."

Wagner recalls that this was typically followed by an outburst of protestation with various people suddenly complaining that they wished to comment, so back to the item they would go.

Early on, taking him aside for a word of advice, Wagner explained to Leslie that discussion in academic circles is typically more measured than elsewhere. One of the reasons was that 'most academics take at least ten seconds to clear their throat.' Leslie took the slap on the wrist in good spirit and soon became more relaxed. Henceforth, the new chairman made sure he waited a longer period for people to speak up and have their say.

Wagner once asked Leslie to consider what he could have achieved if he had had the opportunity for higher education. The question was meant humorously because Leslie's achievements were enormous, but he addressed the question thoughtfully, replying that "thirty minutes at the university was worth a week at the football club in terms of interest and stimulation."

In 1991 Leslie was awarded an Honorary Doctor of Technology in recognition of his services to the community. In September 1992 a decision was made to change the name of Leeds Polytechnic to reflect its new status and, after much discussion, the name Leeds Metropolitan University – rapidly identified by staff and students as Leeds Met or the LMU – was chosen.

In 1998, Leslie announced he was retiring as chairman of the Board of the LMU. By now he was well into his seventies and according to university rules was obliged to retire on the grounds both of age and length of service. However, the LMU had been debating for some time whether to create the post of Chancellor as was customary in such institutions. Many of those with reservations were fearful, not of the post itself but of who might be appointed because, as an honorary post – the Vice-Chancellor was in effect the CEO – it had

After receiving an Honorary
Doctorate in 1991, outside
the Civic Hall

occasionally resulted elsewhere in the appointment of 'celebrities'. It
now became clear that if Leslie had to give up the chairmanship he
could easily become the first Chancellor and still remain involved
with the university. Even those who were opposed in principle to
appointing a Chancellor had no objection to Leslie Silver as a
candidate. As a result, far from opposing his appointment, the notion
was received even by the doubters with enthusiastic acclamation.

At about the same time, LMU had embarked on a major building
project to create an integrated library and computing and media centre
as part of a new front entrance on Woodhouse Lane. The idea that the
building should be named the Leslie Silver Building quickly took root.
There was, however, one person who objected to this proposal – and
that was Leslie Silver himself, who really didn't understand 'what all
the fuss was about'. In due course, and after many discussions, he was
reluctantly persuaded to go along with the proposal.

On Tuesday, 26 October 1999, Leslie became the first Chancellor
of the Leeds Metropolitan University in a special ceremony held at
Leeds Town Hall. The occasion was marked by a formal procession

Installation as Chancellor of
Leeds Metropolitan
University, 26 October
1999, with Vice-Chancellor
Leslie Wagner

The new Chancellor in
front of the Civic Hall

from the Civic Hall to nearby Leeds Town Hall where his friend, and current Vice-Chancellor, Professor Wagner conferred the honour on Leslie. In attendance was George Lascelles, the Earl of Harewood KBE, who gave Leslie's three children an enormous buzz when he introduced their father to the gathering as 'my friend Leslie'.

The proceedings were introduced by Patrick Spens, the new chair of LMU Board of Governors and there was a contribution by Nigel Betts from West Yorkshire Playhouse who gave a reading taken from Jude the Obscure by Thomas Hardy. Simon Lindley, the Leeds City Organist, played music by Francis Jackson and Edward Elgar for the procession and by Henri Mulet for the recession.

In a stirring speech, Leslie thanked the Board of Governors for entrusting him with the post, claiming that he was 'deeply conscious of the responsibility and also the dignity of the office'. He told the assembly that he was a product of the education system of the late 1930s when less than five per cent of the population went on to higher education. "For many of my generation the dole queue was the first option. Our higher education was service in the forces in the Second World War."

Leslie told those present that the explosion of industry and science in the 1950s and 1960s had brought about the need for change and the education system had responded. He pointed out that governments in the sixties had recognised the need for expansion and concentration of vocational and professional higher education. As a consequence the polytechnics, including Leeds, were established and grew rapidly during the seventies. Much remained to be done, he continued, with 35% of young people currently entered into full-time higher education – but the challenge was greater than merely increasing that percentage.

Leslie noted that the university was very much aware of the part it would have to play in shouldering the tasks set out in the Report of the National Committee of Inquiry into Higher Education – popularly known as The Dearing Report – which was published in 1997. "We recognise our responsibility to the city, this region and far beyond, to provide a service that will enable our students to become 'quality citizens' and give them the opportunity to improve their lives as well as the lives of others in their own communities", he said to loud applause.

Leslie also touched upon the changes that had occurred economically and socially since the 1950s and reminded the audience that in the 1950s Leeds was a major manufacturing city, a world leader in the clothing, engineering and printing industries. "Those industries provided significant employment opportunities for young people," he noted. "Today those industries have declined. Instead, Leeds has moved on and now has a thriving, largely service-sector economy, requiring skills in business, finance and computing." The LMU both contributes to, and benefits from, the enormous success of Leeds, he added. "We need Leeds and I believe Leeds needs us".

On a personal note, Leslie described how proud he felt when his eldest daughter Hilary became the first person in his family to go to university in the 1960s. He had always taken great pride in the realisation that all of his grandchildren had either been, or were planning to go to university.

The Vice-Chancellor responded to Leslie's oration by saying that Leslie's contribution to the economic, social and education life of Leeds had been immense. "There can be few others who have enriched the life of so many of its citizens", he noted.

The opening of the Leslie Silver Building at Leeds Metropolitan University, 2000.
Lord Harewood, Nimble Thompson, Leslie and Leslie Wagner

Leslie's role as Chancellor was to act mainly as a figurehead for the University, representing its status, mission and purpose. His duties included presiding over ceremonial occasions, such as the presentation of degrees and honorary degrees, but at all times he remained an advisor to the university.

LMU summer graduation, 2004, with Chief Rabbi Sir Jonathan Sacks and Mrs Sacks

Six

A New
Lease of Life

AFTER ANITA DIED IN 1983, Leslie underwent a long period of adjustment. Without Anita at his side he was at a loss and many members of the family tried to help by keeping him occupied, taking him out socially on numerous occasions.

The first time Leslie met Sheila Harris was at a Leeds United football match. Leslie and Anita had been invited into the LU directors' box as guests of chairman Manny Cussins. As a long time friend of Don Revie and his wife Edna, who lived nearby in Sandmoor Drive, Sheila was accustomed to the privilege of seeing the matches from the exclusive box. It provided the best views of the event as well as corporate hospitality. As Leslie and Anita were proceeding to the Board Room for refreshments at half-time, they bumped into Sheila.

Anita turned to Leslie. "I want you to meet Sheila Harris – she and I go to the same hair stylist", she said with a laugh. Sheila had been widowed for some time. Her late husband Gabby had also been a fervent Leeds United supporter and Leslie had met him previously in a club in London where he was entertaining some customers from overseas. Standing at the bar, Leslie turned around and saw Gabby by his side. He introduced himself as a neighbour – both lived in residences in the north Leeds Sandmoor area. The two men, who had become huge local and national charity benefactors, would continue to meet in Leeds, mostly at fundraising events and quite often at the home of Manny Cussins.

Shortly after Anita had died, Sheila Silver, the wife of Leslie's cousin David, from Manchester, came over to Leeds and Leslie took her out for a meal at the Flying Pizza on Street Lane. Sheila Harris was also dining there with her brother-in-law, Eli Harris. Seeing Leslie from a distance, she came over to his table and offered condolences and sympathy on the loss of Anita. The trio chatted for a short while and Leslie made the introductions. Sheila Harris asked Leslie if he would be going to Elland Road and suggested that the two of them should meet up there at some point in the future.

London-born Sheila Harris (née Benson) had come to Leeds during World War Two and had spent two years at Leeds College of Art. She was effervescent, bright and full of life and Leslie was impressed. After she returned to her restaurant table Leslie's relative, noticing his interest, leaned closer to Leslie and whispered: "She's extremely vivacious, isn't she? Do you know what I think Leslie; one day you'll marry that woman."

Leslie just smiled and didn't give the matter much thought until, after several weeks had elapsed, Sheila Harris popped into his mind and he decided to phone her. He said he would like to take her up on her suggestion and accompany her to a football match as his guest in the directors' box. Sheila said she would be delighted to accept and that afternoon Leslie realised that this would accelerate his healing process. It was the beginning of a deep and lasting friendship.

Since Anita's death Leslie, now in his mid-fifties, had suffered from loneliness and Sheila filled an enormous gap. She was warm, with an enchanting smile and consequently extremely good company. Her sparkling personality brought out the best in him and, with her own two sons Raymond and Brian, he had a new circle of people to occupy him.

Leslie's children were wary at first but soon warmed to Sheila's appeal. From Leslie's perspective he thought it was 'useful for anyone's dear old dad to be looked after by someone else, especially if that person really loved him'.

There was no official engagement but close-on fifteen months after Anita's death, Leslie and Sheila married on 29 April 1984, under a canopy in her garden in Sandmoor Drive. The service was conducted by Dr Rabbi Solomon Brown from the United Hebrew Congregation, a renowned rabbi both parties admired and respected. A small family reception followed and the couple then set off on a cruise to South Africa travelling by train from Cape Town to Johannesburg before

Wedding of
Leslie to
Sheila Harris,
29 April 1984

going on safari. Sheila's interests were completely different from
those of Anita. She was outgoing and delighted in an active social
life. Surprisingly, she was not a public speaker – that was something
she left to Leslie. Over a period of time, Sheila, who loved visiting
Elland Road, had made a lot of contacts in the football world. The
beautiful game had its compensations and she readily enjoyed the
lifestyle it provided.

A leisure pursuit that Leslie was fond of, but compelled to drop,
was playing Bridge which Anita had loved and at which she was
highly proficient. The game, alas, did not appeal to his new wife. As
a member of Moor Allerton Golf Club, Leslie played golf when the

opportunity arose, which was mainly on a Sunday, but that wasn't very often. Nevertheless, one of the many things the couple had in common was a love of travelling and they embarked on a series of cruises and luxury holidays. Apart from sightseeing, Sheila also adored shopping and doing serious damage to her and Leslie's credit cards.

The couple lived initially at Leslie's home in Sandmoor Avenue, but after a few months they came to the decision to start afresh in a home of their own. Bracken Park Lodge on Syke Lane had come on the market in 1984. The house, set in some fifteen acres of land, had originally belonged to Leslie's old supermarket chum and customer Barry Baker and Leslie struck a deal with its present owner, David Richmond. Sheila inspected the interior decoration and her creative juices began to flow; she was itching to put her mark on the residence. With her meticulous eye for detail, she converted the swimming pool

10th wedding anniversary family group, 1994
Back row: Mark Silver, Raymond Harris, Gabrielle Harris , Donald Komrower, Adam Komrower, Brian Harris, Justin Harris, Sheila Silver, Leslie Silver, Jenny Komrower, Lisa Brosh, Talya Brosh, Karen Brosh.
Seated: Daniel Komrower, Jane Komrower, Carol Harris, Holly Harris, Hilary Brosh, Hannah Silver, Tina Silver, Alexandra Silver

Leslie celebrating his 75th birthday with a
party at Harewood House, 2000
above - with his children
below - with his grandchildren

into an indoor functions facility, adding a snooker room for Leslie and refurbishing the four bedrooms and renovating the en-suite amenities. The house had a generously proportioned foyer which was used for receptions and a spacious lounge and dining area that, together with a modern kitchen, made the residence a comfortable house with a knock-out factor. The garden and lawns were beautifully landscaped and Leslie became very attached to the pond with lots of exotic fish swimming around. It was an ideal property for entertaining, a vibrant place to live, and both families loved to visit.

For many years to come it became the idyllic setting for many fund-raising events. In the beautiful surroundings and gardens many people from different backgrounds and walks of life descended on Bracken Park Lodge to raise money as well as their glasses of champagne cocktails and to enjoy the view while snacking on impeccably catered nibbles.

A TERRIBLE ORDEAL

One evening in March 1996, Sheila and Leslie were at home in the downstairs lounge at 9.30pm watching television when they were to endure a terrifying experience which was to change their lives forever. The couple suddenly heard footsteps on the staircase and three masked men swiftly burst into the room. They ordered Leslie and Sheila to kneel on the carpet face downwards with strict instructions not to look at them. A blanket, which the trespassers had taken from the master bedroom when they broke into the property, was thrown over them after the couple were made to hand over spare cash.

Leslie was blindfolded and then handcuffed to the knob of a door in the snooker-room while Sheila was the one the balaclava-clad intruders chose to be their guide, forcing her to show them the location of the house safes. One of the men, slim-built, in his mid-twenties and over six feet tall, said that they knew the Silvers had two house safes and that it was jewellery they were after. Sheila was ordered to hand over the keys to the safe where over £200,000 of her gem collection was kept. They then proceeded to remove every item – rings, bracelets, pearls, watches and baubles – stashing the haul into a bag and leaving the keys to the handcuffs on the nearby fireplace before making their exit.

For a few moments the place seemed lifeless as both Leslie and Sheila were understandably traumatised. The incident had happened so suddenly, and had left them in a stunned silence. After much struggling, Leslie was able to reach the phone and managed to dial 999. All in all, the incident lasted no more than twenty minutes, but as Leslie recalled later, it seemed like twenty years and for many months the pair had flashbacks and numerous nightmares about what had occurred and what might have happened.

In most dramatic incidents there is a flicker of humour and there had been such a moment that Sheila and Leslie always fell back on when recalling the horrendous ordeal to friends and family. It was a light-hearted incident worthy of Inspector Clouseau himself because when the police eventually arrived some minutes later, they very politely rang the front door bell to gain entrance. Leslie shouted through the letter box that as the house keys had been taken by the intruders, the police would have to enter the premises the same way that the burglars did – through the upstairs bedroom window. The detective inspector responded by lifting up the letter box flap and shouting back "Thanks for the heads-up, sir".

The jewellery was never recovered and the culprits, who were professionals and reasonably quiet in deed and manner, knew exactly what they wanted. They were never apprehended, which often worried Sheila and Leslie. However, Sheila did recover the value of the jewellery through her insurance and, according to Leslie, to offset the trauma of the ordeal went out and 'spent the bloody lot.'

It was an atrocious misfortune and for the following months the pair lost faith in everything, continually feeling nervous, anxious and insecure. A good night's sleep was out of the question for both of them, and for some time Leslie hired a security man to guard the house. Accommodation was found for him in the spacious garage from where he would watch the house evening and night.

Apparently Leslie, still chairman of Leeds United at the time, had been just one of many footballers and managers that had been targeted at that time in some rather daring house robberies. Nevertheless, the incident had taken the edge off Leslie's confidence and, in conjunction with a deterioration in his health, planted the seed in his mind to step down as chairman. Something that annoyed Leslie was an incident that occurred in the Board Room at

Elland Road some time after the robbery. One of the police chiefs that had been working on the case approached Leslie and, referring to the unsolved crime, told him that although the police knew who had committed the felony, there was insufficient evidence to charge them.

In 2005, Leslie and Sheila decided to sell Bracken Park Lodge after two blissful decades marred only by the traumatic break-in. They wanted to downsize and chose a penthouse apartment in The Moorings on Harrogate Road. Life became more relaxed again and apart from holidays the couple delighted in the Leeds community's many social and charitable events where there was always top-table, red-carpet treatment awaiting them, much to Leslie's constant cry of not understanding 'what all the fuss was about'.

PHILANTHROPY

Leslie's philanthropy is legendary and his approach to submitting a refusal to a charitable appeal is to send a sizeable cheque. Paying a visit to Professor Wagner in his office in the mid-1990s, Leslie's mood was extremely dejected. He had spent a whole afternoon attempting unsuccessfully to raise funds for a children's cancer charity.

Sitting down with a sigh, he told his friend that he had visited a number of Yorkshire millionaires, of whom there were a considerable number, but had been offered pitiful sums. In the course of bemoaning his failure, Leslie asked his friend: "What do these people do with all their money?" After pondering his own question for a few seconds, Leslie amused Professor Wagner by answering the question himself. "Unless you have a mistress or an art collection surely you can't spend more than £250,000 a year," he said sincerely. It was a lovely Leslie Silver moment.

Leslie's charity work knew no bounds. He was a supporter and benefactor of the Leeds Society for Deaf and Blind People, a long-established charity committed to meeting the needs of people with sensory loss. The charity once needed a significant sum to match-fund a three-year project to provide communicator guides for deaf-blind people. There was uncertainty whether the local authority would provide funding, but in order that services could continue Leslie gave a three-year commitment for the funds. As it turned out, the local authority eventually provided the funds, but as an indication

Presenting a cheque to the Variety Club for the Children's Radiology Unit, April 2010.
With Ian Brill, Bobby Caplin OBE, Maggie Boyle, David Wilson, Chairman of Yorkshire
Region of the Variety Club, Leslie and Sheila Silver.

of Leslie's generosity he maintained his original commitment,
enabling the society to develop its services in other areas.

Leslie contributed substantial sums of money directly to support
the research carried out by Cancer Research UK, principally in
Leeds, but his contacts were national as well. He worked tirelessly
to make contacts between cancer research in Yorkshire and research
nationally with other potential major donors, using his influence
and reputation to promote major donations. His work was also
instrumental in fundraising to support the major developments
in facilities within the University of Leeds and the Leeds Teaching
Hospitals NHS Trust.

Emmaus, a Leeds charity to help homeless people, was launched
in the late 1990s. Leslie was approached with a request that he
might utilise his charitable trust to support the start-up costs.
Needless to say, Leslie willingly agreed and arranged to donate two
tranches of funding.

Variety, the children's charity, has been privileged to count on
Leslie as one of its major donors over several decades. With his help,
the charity was able to provide Sunshine coaches and electric
wheelchairs in order to improve the lives of less fortunate children.

In 2007, the charity honoured him with a lifetime achievement award at a luncheon at the Queen's Hotel. In April, 2010 a new children's radiology unit was created at the Leeds General Infirmary thanks to a £250,000 cash injection. This donation stemmed from Variety, the children's charity, and included £125,000 donation from Leslie. The unit, based at the Clarendon Wing, provides scans using imaging technology to diagnose and treat sick youngsters. It boasts state-of-the-art equipment which reduces the dosage of X-rays so is quicker and alleviates anxiety for children and parents, enabling results to be available swiftly.

Leslie has always been willing to support the arts as well as sciences. In the 1980s, for example, Leeds Playhouse launched an appeal to build a new theatre. Fundraisers needed one big donation to kick-start the appeal. Leslie not only gave a substantial sum of money but he then took the chair of a development committee set up to raise the rest.

Leslie's philanthropy had particular hallmarks. He always worked modestly and quietly without ever seeking to attract attention to his own efforts or contributions. His commitment, integrity and altruism always came across clearly and he had great knowledge and understanding of issues concerned with science and fundraising. Unlike most multi-millionaires Leslie remained true to his socialist beliefs. Although Leslie's philanthropy has been too widely dispensed to permit coverage of every aspect, a further couple of individual projects are worthy of particular note.

Donisthorpe Hall

Leslie held an interest in elderly residential care and developed a fondness and admiration for the Leeds care home at Donisthorpe Hall, which had been founded in 1923 under the name Leeds Home for Aged Jews and Home of Rest in Cowper Street just off Chapeltown Road. In 1956, the home moved to a considerable estate in Moortown called Donisthorpe Hall and proved to be a sizeable and much valued facility for the Jewish community in Leeds.

The years progressed but unfortunately Donisthorpe did not, and although kindness and care continued to be administered, the surroundings and interiors had a neglected air about them. In 2003, Geoff Caplan, who was the care home's new finance director, realised that things were not moving forward as they should, but what was to be done? After a close examination of the books, he discovered that £6 million had been invested in the home's bank account, but since the home was losing about £600,000 a year, with the loss just covered by investment income, the home was barely breaking even and unable to progress. Geoff had noted an undeveloped area adjoining Donisthorpe Hall which belonged to the charity. The obvious thing to do, he felt, was to build a brand new unit there which over the years would enable them to decant residents from the old part to the new and free up space in the old building. In fact it proved to be a solid blueprint for forward thinking and sensible planning.

The then chairman, Sam Goldman, a stalwart and dedicated supporter, came from a generation whose adage was to set aside a large reserve for 'a rainy day', resulting in the build up of a substantial capital sum. The committee, headed by Geoff, put it to him as follows: "Sam, the rainy day is here. In fact, it's pouring down and we are getting soaked to the skin."

After a lot of acrimonious meetings and much throwing of new ideas into and out of the ring, Sam capitulated. But there were further disputes because Sam wanted to build an eighty-bed unit which the Trustees thought would just replicate the small and cramped conditions associated with the status quo. Their preference was to make Donisthorpe Hall a modern en-suite, purpose-built, state-of-the-art residential care home with the aim of promoting it as one of the best care homes in the country.

After consultations with architects, who were many times sent back to their drawing boards, the project was changed to include a forty-bed en-suite unit presenting residents with more space and much improved facilities. However, the home's executives were in need of a key donor who would help the initiative along and give it some kudos.

Sam had known Leslie for many years and approached him with the intention of obtaining a substantial donation. He told him that Geoff Caplan 'and his mob' were driving him crazy with plans for the care home to receive a modern make-over. Leslie, of course, was all for the investment – in order to succeed and run efficiently one had to keep up with the times. Consequently, being ready, willing and able to help, he did so by making a £250,000 donation. The building committee now had the requisite backing to green-light the project and the new wing, named Silver Lodge, was built, creating a massive turnaround for Donisthorpe Hall. Leslie, being Leslie, certainly didn't want a lot of kudos about Silver Lodge and gave the caveat: "Please remember, I don't want any fuss," However, he did agree to dig the first sod on the site and when the unit was completed he and Sheila came along to open it – but Leslie still didn't know what all the fuss was about.

Without a doubt, Leslie's contribution made a huge difference and opened the gates for further developments including the building of a vital Alzheimer's unit, a sun room and extensive renovations. Dementia had suddenly become the new cancer disease, often spoken of in hushed tones. A terrible disease affecting the growing ageing population, there is no cure and the home was admitting more and more cases. This eventually led to more improvements and the building of more units for dementia sufferers with trained staff being brought in to cope with the influx.

ॐ ॐ ॐ

The Shadwell Lane care home has always had a soft spot for Leslie and his family, and in January 2015 they held a tea party in his honour to celebrate his ninetieth birthday.

Cutting the sod to start building
Silver Lodge at Donisthorpe Hall
in 2002

With Chief Rabbi
Ephraim Mirvis at
Donisthorpe Hall, 2014

Jewish National Fund (JNF)

By his own admission, Leslie is not a religious man, but he is Jewish in thought and deed. Every Rosh Hashanah (Jewish New Year) and Yom Kippur (Day of Atonement) he would take his place in synagogue, at the United Hebrew Congregation in Shadwell Lane, which he did largely out of respect for, and in memory of, his dearly loved parents, Harry and Bessie. "It was as if he used these dates as a special *Yahrzeit* for them", Professor Wagner was to observe.

On Wagner's retirement from the LMU in 2003, the Leeds branch of the Jewish National Fund (JNF) held a fund-raising tribute dinner in his honour, which Leslie and Sheila sponsored. The main purpose of JNF annual dinners, needless to say, was to rake in money for JNF projects in Israel. Wagner was interested to hear whether Leslie had ever been honoured in this way in the past. It transpired that he had not, and when Wagner enquired of JNF officials why this had not occurred, he was advised to 'ask Leslie', which he proceeded to do. Reluctant at first to admit the reason, Leslie would shrug his shoulders and prevaricate, but after some persistent questioning he admitted that he had been approached many years previously. In truth, he confessed, he had declined on the grounds that for the umpteenth time, he didn't want to be in the limelight.

JNF organisers had explained to Leslie that as well as honouring him the dinner was intended to raise substantial funds for a special project in Israel. "So how much are you expecting to make?" Leslie enquired. When they told him the amount Leslie sat down, produced his cheque book and proceeded to write a cheque for the stated sum. "Here you are", he said, handing over the piece of paper, "now you don't need to make a dinner."

A TRAGIC SETBACK

In the autumn of 2012, Sheila began complaining of urinary problems which had become very uncomfortable. As a result, her GP referred her to a specialist at The Spire private hospital in Roundhay. He recommended that she have a scan which resulted in her being told she had an early-stage cancer in one of the kidneys. She was shocked by the diagnosis but in some way comforted by being informed that the problem was treatable. But despite a few weeks of medication and rest, the problem persisted and soon became more aggressive.

In early 2013 she was sent back to the hospital for a second scan. Returning to the consultant's rooms some days later, Leslie and Sheila anxiously waited for the result, which proved to be a most devastating experience for the whole family. Facing the consultant were Leslie, Sheila and her son Raymond. The consultant took his seat and said quietly: "I have to tell you, Mrs Silver, that we have done a wide-spread scan and you have cancer all over your body – I'm afraid there is nothing we can do about it." Sheila drew in a sharp intake of breath. Leslie was disbelieving and Raymond was visibly upset. After a moment Leslie asked the consultant to repeat the prognosis which he did.

Although undeniably shocked, Sheila was stoical and reacted in a quiet and dignified manner, appearing to take the news firmly on the chin. She was admitted to hospital for a week but on returning home she became severely ill. Leslie tried not to tread too heavily around the apartment. She was in a huge amount of pain and as the weeks progressed her condition deteriorated.

In April 2013, after much suffering, bravely borne, Sheila died, leaving Leslie and her sons bereft.

During the nights of *Shiva* (mourning), the Jewish community poured into the apartment to mourn with the family and to offer to

Leslie, his family and Sheila's two sons and their families, sympathy and condolences. Leslie's loss and pain were evident and family and friends felt deeply for him. He was a man acquainted with grief having outlived two wives after two long and very happy marriages, but over the ensuing weeks Leslie slowly managed to come round and gain some sort of composure, with enormous help from Hilary whom he was to describe later as 'my rock'. His elder daughter was always one jump ahead of her father and continually thinking of ways to keep him occupied, to meet old friends or make new ones that would interest him and keep her family diverted.

A much needed distraction came in September 2013 when Leslie was among the many recipients of a new award for veterans of the RAF's Bomber Command campaigns of the Second World War. Hilary had seen an announcement in the media requesting veterans and relatives to come forward and write in with more information.

The bravery of men in Bomber Command was never recognised by the British government until a review was set in motion in 2012. The clasp is granted to the aircrew of Bomber Command who served for at least sixty days or completed a tour of operations on a bomber command operational unit and flew at least one operational sortie on a bomber. Leslie received the Bomber Command Clasp in recognition of his contribution – he had taken part in some forty operations in Europe and twenty in the Far East.

More than 50,000 men died while flying with Bomber Command during the war. As the news of the Bomber Command Clasp award became public, Leslie was as modest as usual and told Hilary that the award was 'very nice', but he was honoured nevertheless. It had never occurred to him, a man now in his late eighties, that he had lived at the heart of history, yet this award suddenly brought the past closer to the future and his eyes filled with tears. In typically modest fashion, his first reaction was to think of lost comrades.

"At that time people were basically anti-fascist and wanted to fight back. We were very focussed on the job so there was no time for fear", he said.

Caressing the award, he said to Hilary: "It brings back memories of some very fine fellows who sadly didn't get back. What it amounts to, though, is that I had a job to do and had mates who I was very close to. I believed in my capabilities."

Receipt of the Bomber Command Clasp, September 2013
Leslie at home with Hilary

Seven

A Life Worth Celebrating

A LIFE WORTHY OF CELEBRATION could very well sum up the achievements of an exceptional man. Leslie Silver OBE has become, through hard work, loyalty and integrity, a truly remarkable son of Leeds, a city that he adopted when he arrived as a teenager from London in the late 1940s. Even now he still remembers the love and importance of family life that he experienced in the East End. Though they are spread over three continents, he surveys with huge pride and love all of his eleven grandchildren and thirteen great-grandchildren, keeping in touch by phone calls, emails, shared photographs and cherished visits.

At a family gathering in November 2013 at Stoke Park Hotel in Buckinghamshire, thirty-two members of his immediate family got together – only Jane and her son-in-law Joey were unable to attend.

A poignant toast was drunk to the memory of Leslie's grandfather Isaac Meyer Silverstein, whose decision to leave Poland all those decades ago was the trigger for this family reunion. Many of Leslie's qualities stem from his working class, left-wing background. He has been a robust innovator and an ardent champion of higher education. He has always spoken out against racial and social injustice with a plea for fair play whenever he sees discrimination and intolerance rear its ugly head.

What Leslie's grandparents would have made of it all is an interesting speculation. As penniless immigrants they would obviously have wanted their descendents to aspire to greater glories, but it seems unlikely that they could have taken on board the possibility of a grandchild becoming a multi-millionaire industrialist, philanthropist and holder of many positions of importance to the wider community.

For his part Leslie enjoyed particular satisfaction from pulling Leeds United out of the Second Division and he was a man on a mission when it came to enabling young people to achieve their maximum potential through higher education. Throughout his life there has always been soccer. As an eight-year-old watching from the terraces at Highbury, it was all about the famous Arsenal heroes, Hapgood and Bastin, but once the war was out of the way it was about the old dirt kop at Elland Road and players like Wakefield, Cochrane, Kerfoot and Dunn and a young player called John Charles. After he became Leeds United chairman football suddenly became a different game. "We had seen a great club going into a slow decline and the opportunity of assisting in trying to put it back at the top was a great challenge," Leslie said in 1983.

Above all he loves the city of Leeds with an abiding passion. At some point or another during his life Leslie has been associated with almost every significant organisation. He has made a major contribution to the life and culture of Leeds through his involvement with the West Yorkshire Playhouse, Leeds City Art Gallery, Radio Aire, the paint industry and most famously his beloved Leeds United Football Club which he chaired for twelve years. From the humble beginnings in an old converted stable in 1946, his paint company had, by 1991, recorded a turnover of £100 million and was located in large, state-of-the-art premises just outside Leeds.

Leslie Silver OBE gives without conditions attached and without asking for personal reward. Informed on one occasion by an admirer that his liberal humanism had contributed greatly to the city where he made his mark and that he had given a lot to Leeds, his reply was typically Leslie: "On the contrary, Leeds has given a lot to me."

When all is said and done, Leslie's greatest accomplishment is arguably to have held so many positions of influence without making enemies. Leslie Wagner never ceased to be amazed by Leslie's popularity. During degree days at Leeds Town Hall, and in between ceremonies, he and Leslie used to walk back together to the Vice-Chancellor's office. On every occasion it was guaranteed that the men would be stopped in the street by people wanting to greet Leslie.

Many were former Kalon employees happy to see their former boss, but most were just members of the wider public eager to offer their good wishes. Leslie, a hero to his own community, needless to say took the meetings and greetings in his stride.

Even at the time of writing this book to celebrate Leslie's 90th birthday, an achievement in itself for a man of his generation, Leslie remains a recognised and popular figure. Although he now largely shuns the limelight, his favourite place, other than watching football in his apartment with a dram of whisky by his side, is sitting at the table immediately inside the entrance to the Amici restaurant, an eatery a stone's throw away on Harrogate Road. There in the company of family members and friends he is constantly approached by well-wishers, often from a long time in his past. He neither is, nor ever will be forgotten.

A family weekend at Stoke Park, December 2013
Back row: Vikki Komrower, Daniel Komrower, Helen Komrower, Adam Komrower, Alex Silver, Tom Whittaker, Hannah Silver, Karen Brosh, Mark Silver, Ben Kingston, Talya Kingston, Lisa King, Joshua King, Ben Silver.
Seated: Chris Kingston, Cara Kingston, Tina Silver, Leslie, Hilary Curwen, Peter Curwen, Jenny Renju, Maisie Silver, Rosie Silver. (Jane Komrower and Joey Renju were abroad and unable to attend)

Silver Family Tree

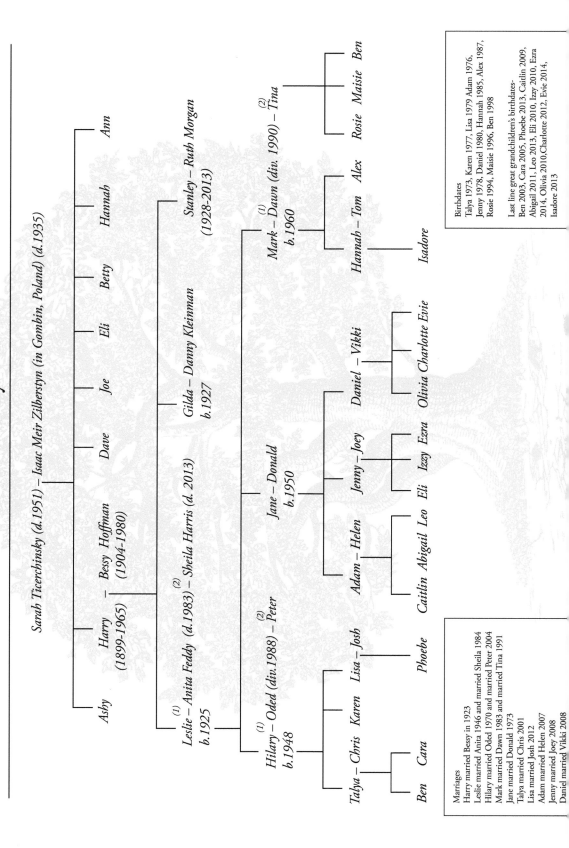

Sarah Ticerchinsky (d.1951) – Isaac Meir Zilberstyn (in Gombin, Poland) (d.1935)

Ashy   Harry – Bessy Hoffman   Dave   Joe   Eli   Betty   Hannah   Ann
        (1899-1965) (1904-1980)

Leslie – Anita Feddy (d.1983) ⁽²⁾ Sheila Harris (d. 2013)   Gilda – Danny Kleinman   Stanley – Ruth Morgan
b.1925   b.1927   (1928-2013)

Hilary – Oded (div. 1988) ⁽²⁾ Peter   Jane – Donald   Mark – Dawn (div. 1990) ⁽²⁾ Tina
b.1948   b.1950   b.1960

Talya – Chris   Karen   Lisa – Josh   Phoebe   Adam – Helen   Jenny – Joey   Daniel – Vikki   Hannah – Tom   Alex   Rosie   Maisie   Ben

Ben   Cara   Caitlin Abigail Leo Eli   Izzy Ezra   Olivia Charlotte Evie   Isadore

Marriages
Harry married Bessy in 1923
Leslie married Anita 1946 and married Sheila 1984
Hilary married Oded 1970 and married Peter 2004
Mark married Dawn 1983 and married Tina 1991
Jane married Donald 1973
Talya married Chris 2001
Lisa married Josh 2012
Adam married Helen 2007
Jenny married Joey 2008
Daniel married Vikki 2008

Birthdates
Talya 1973, Karen 1977, Lisa 1979 Adam 1976,
Jenny 1978, Daniel 1980, Hannah 1985, Alex 1987,
Rosie 1994, Maisie 1996, Ben 1998

Last line great grandchildren's birthdates-
Ben 2003, Cara 2005, Phoebe 2013, Caitlin 2009,
Abigail 2011, Leo 2013, Eli 2010, Izzy 2010, Ezra
2014, Olivia 2010,Charlotte 2012, Evie 2014,
Isadore 2013

Appendix

Where are they now?

When Leslie's uncle Ashy moved to Manchester it seemed like a move to a foreign land. Now, Leslie's family really is in foreign lands, dispersed over three continents; Europe, Africa and the USA. It includes two medical doctors, three doctorates, three professors, two international hoteliers, and a brewer!

Hilary is still in Leeds, Karen, Lisa and family are in London and Talya and family live in Amherst, Massachusetts, US. Jane lives in Hampshire next door to Adam and family, Daniel and family are in Liverpool and Jenny and family are in Moshi, Tanzania. Mark and his family live in Mougins in the South of France, two of his daughters are in Boston, Massachusetts at university and two in London. The family story in a sense came full circle when Hannah Silver moved to live in the East End of London, before moving with her family to Dalston.

Kalon Group is now PPG Architectural Coatings UK Ltd, part of American company PPG Industries. In 2013 it showed sales of $15 billion. PPG's Birstall plant in Huddersfield Road still houses Europe's largest manufacturing facility for decorative paint.

ટે ટે ટે

In 2013 it was announced that the Board of Governors had applied to the privy council to change the name of Leeds Metropolitan University to Leeds Beckett University, after the location of one of the university's founding colleges, Beckett Park, which in turn was named after Ernest Beckett, 2nd Baron Grimthorpe.

The name change, after protests amongst students, became official in September 2014.

And as for Leeds United FC, well, the least said about that the better, although Leslie sings the team song Marching on Together every home game he attends. The team has had its ups and downs, but mainly downs. Currently languishing in the middle of the Championship League with little hope of enjoying again the success they had under Leslie's watch, he is happy to support them and paint over the cracks.

Index

... of people & organisations

INDEX